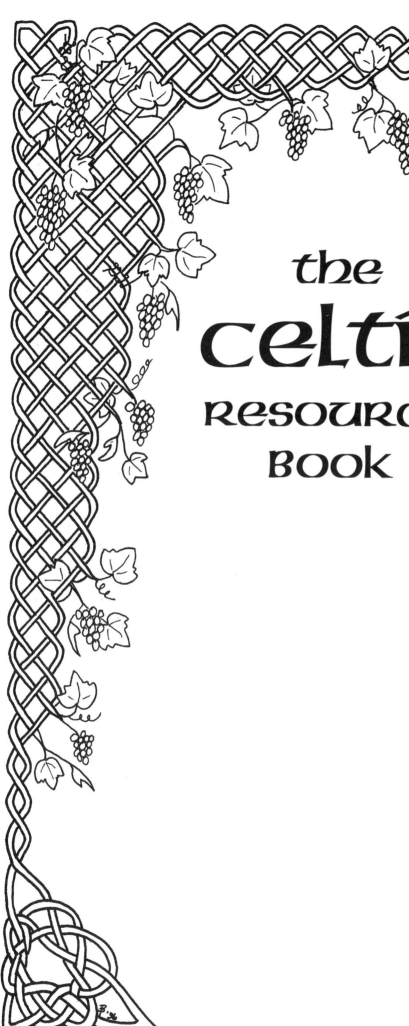

the
celtic
resource
book

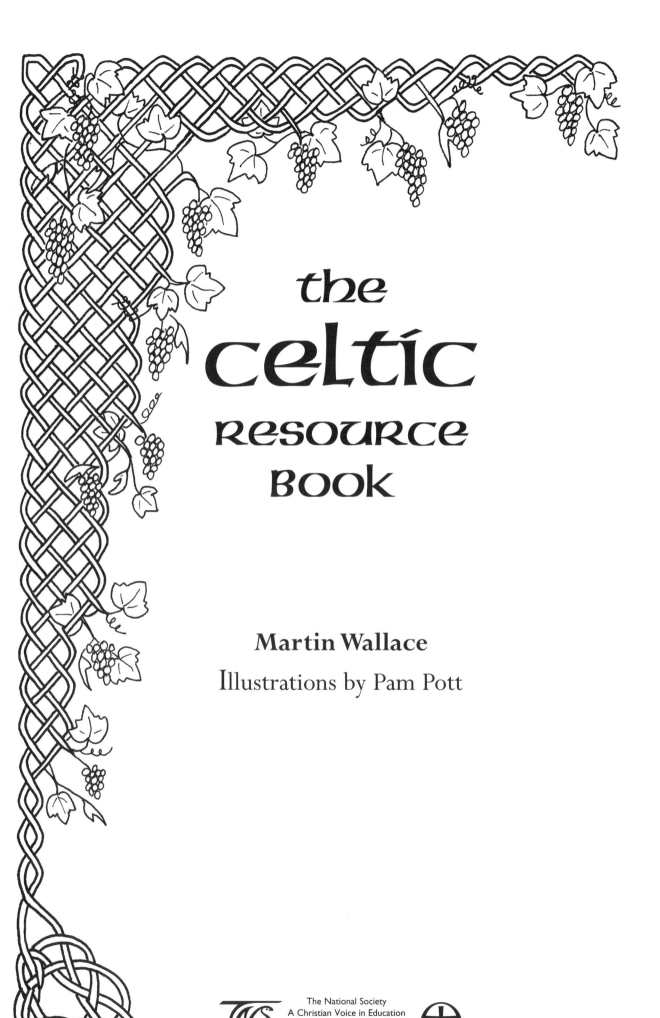

the
CeLtíc
Resource
Book

Martin Wallace

Illustrations by Pam Pott

The National Society
A Christian Voice in Education

a co-publication with
Church House Publishing

National Society/Church House Publishing,
Church House,
Great Smith Street,
London SW1P 3NZ

ISBN 0 7151 4906 7

Published 1998 by The National Society/Church House Publishing

Cover design by Julian Smith

Printed in England by Biddles Ltd, Guildford and King's Lynn

contents

This book is dedicated
to all those people
who have been fellow pilgrims
along the Celtic Trail
at St Peter's Chapel at Bradwell in Essex.

acknowledgements

During the summers of 1994–7 in that isolated Celtic chapel of St Peter, Bradwell, built by St Cedd of Lindisfarne in AD 654, we enjoyed an exploration into the unknown. Each Sunday, evening services were held which combined gentle Irish and Scottish music, prayers from Lindisfarne, songs from Iona, and challenging sermons based on insights from the Celtic saints. In a chapel which could hold 60 comfortably, there might be anything up to 250 people, many of whom had driven for an hour to be present. During those occasions, as people sat on hard wooden benches, the peace was such that a pin could be heard to drop. The silence was expectant. Those who came were Christians of all denominations, and they brought their friends of no faith too. The appreciative comments were both surprising and astonishing. It seemed this style and content were reaching depths of the soul previously unplumbed.

My thanks go to those musicians from Bradwell, especially Laurie and Brigid Main, and Val Butler, who were fellow travellers into the unknown, bringing harmony with their instruments and voices. Those who faithfully came week after week in ever-increasing numbers and regularity were an inspiration, and it was from among them that the suggestion first came to make the material more widely available.

Each July an ecumenical pilgrimage occurs at Bradwell. In 1997 5,000 arrived to enjoy the Celtic elements in the open-air worship, and to try their hand at various Celtic artistic activities. Many of the activities in this book are derived from ventures tried either at the pilgrimage or at the many workshops, retreats and quiet days held each year around the country. About 2,000 people each year were reached by these events, and my heartfelt thanks go to those who showed that such activities were not only fun but also valuable in developing spiritual insights. Special thanks go to Annie Mawson who plays her harps and sings in such a wonderfully atmospheric way, that her contribution transforms many of the events.

I am indebted to Sallie Nightingale who typed the earlier part of this book and to Julie Medhurst who completed the lion's share of that work. Other friends who have contributed, areas where my own knowledge and experience is severely limited include Fran Wakefield, Hazel Palmer, Val Butler, Glenda Abbott, Joan Houghton, Rosemary Power, Adrian Leighton, and my daughter Caroline Wallace. Pam Pott deserves a special mention for her glorious artwork. I am also grateful to Amelia Beane, James Ayton, John Davies, Joanna Stephens, Ramon Beeching and Beth Rogers who have given permission for their prayers to be reproduced.

These events and people are mentioned with real gratitude and to underline the fact that Celtic pilgrimage is not a lonely trek, but rather a wonderful corporate journey which involves drawing closer to other people, to one's own soul, and to the loving heart of God. May these resources make that true for all who use them.

Martin Wallace

Acknowledgements

The author and publisher gratefully acknowledge permission to reproduce copyright material in this book. Every effort has been made to trace owners of copyright material and the author apologises for any inadvertent omissions. Information about such omissions should be sent to the publisher, who will make full acknowledgement in future editions.

Church of Scotland Panel on Worship 1997, *Pray Now – A Pattern of Daily Devotions*, 1997-8:
p. 18 Lord, stretch out towards those who cannot pray
p. 21 O Lord of all creation
p. 26 There are times when I feel happy
p. 59 I have had enough

Church House Publishing, *Pocket Celtic Prayers*, edited by Martin Wallace, 1996:
p. 79 God who made us, we worship you (by Daphne Bridges)
p. 79 God the creator, renew this plant's growth (by Daphne Bridges)
p. 171 Three things are pleasant in a home (by Janet Donaldson)

Community of Aidan and Hilda, *Resources for Worship in the Celtic Tradition*, 1995:
p. 35 In the name of the all-powerful Father
p. 40 With these hands I bless the lonely
p. 45 We offer You
p. 46 Creator Spirit, come
p. 46 Spirit of God

Darton, Longman and Todd, *Celtic Fire*, by Robert Van de Weyer, 1990:
p. 56 Delightful it is to stand on the peak of a rock
p. 57 I wish, ancient and eternal King
p. 58 I am the wind that breathes upon the sea
p. 76 Remember the poor when you look out on fields you own

Floris Books, *Carmina Gadelica*, by Alexander Carmichael, 1992:
p. 19 I am bending my knee
p. 20 Bless to me, O God
p. 21 Thanks to you, O God
p. 27 I believe, O God of all gods
p. 30 In name of God
p. 31 A wavelet for your form
p. 31 A small drop of water
p. 35 I am going home with you
p. 38 May the eye of the great God
p. 38 God's grace distil on you
p. 39 The love and affection of the angels be to you
p. 40 The guarding of the God of life be upon me
p. 40 The sacred three
p. 49 Bless, O God, my little cow
p. 60 Come I this day to the Father

p. 60 God be with thee in every pass
p. 61 My walk this day with God
p. 62 Bless to me, O God
p. 64 Be Christ's cross on your new dwelling
p. 64 I smoor the fire this night
p. 66 The peace of God, the peace of men
p. 66 O God, bless my homestead
p. 68 Be with me, O God, at the breaking of bread
p. 69 O King of stars!
p. 70 May the Light of lights come
p. 71 I lie down this night with God
p. 72 May I speak this day according to Thy justice
p. 72 On the holy Sunday of Thy God
p. 73 O God, who broughtst me from the rest of last night
p. 73 The eye of the great God
p. 75 Be Thou with us, O Chief of chiefs

Hodder and Stoughton, *Celtic Worship through the Year*, by Ray Simpson, 1997:
p. 18 May Sunday be a day of resurrection
p. 26 The glory of God in my working
p. 29 The Father is always present
p. 32 Peace in your thinking

Hodder and Stoughton, *Exploring Celtic Spirituality*, by Ray Simpson, 1995:
p. 77 Call, Call, Call, great Chief of the high hills

Kevin Mayhew Ltd, *Be Still*, by Susan Sayers, 1996, used by permission. Licence Nos. 892061 and 896030:
p. 22 Shadows lengthen
p. 23 Through our nights and days
p. 27 Wherever you call us, Lord, our God

Marshall Pickering, HarperCollins, *Celtic Daily Prayer*, The Northumbria Community, 1994:
p. 37 May the peace of the Lord Christ go with you

Marshall Pickering, HarperCollins, *Celtic Night Prayer*, The Northumbria Community, 1996:
p. 19 As the tide draws the waters
p. 29 Lord, let our memory
p. 32 God bless your house
p. 68 Bless, O Lord

Marshall Pickering, HarperCollins, *Book of a Thousand Prayers*, edited by Angela Ashwin, 1996:
p. 34 Into the darkness (by Ruth Burgess)

SPCK, *The Edge of Glory*, by David Adam, 1985:

p. 64 God give grace

p. 65 Peace be in my life

p. 65 The Father is in the house

p. 66 God bless this house from roof to floor

p. 67 Bless the father of this house

p. 74 I give my hands to you Lord

SPCK, *Border Lands*, by David Adam, 1991:

p. 20 God of the dawning

p. 32 Lord, today brings

p. 32 Come Lord, come light, come love

p. 43 I open the stable door

p. 44 The Lord of the empty tomb

p. 45 The Cross of Christ

p. 47 When I feel alone

p. 48 You are the Maker

p. 49 Where the mist rises from the sea

SPCK, *Power Lines*, by David Adam, 1992:

p. 76 Grant us a vision, Lord

p. 77 Lord, reveal in us your glory

p. 77 Lord, whatever we build

SPCK, *The Rhythm of Life*, by David Adam, 1996:

p. 42 Jesus, born a refugee

p. 44 By your death upon the cross

United Reform Church, *Encompassing Presence*, by
Kate Mcllhagga, 1993:

p. 18 Bright shining star

p. 21 Thanks be to you, O God

The Wild Goose Resource Group,
Iona Community, Glasgow G51 3UV,
Scotland, *The Wee Worship Book*, 1991:

p. 20 O God, you summon the day to dawn

p. 22 Come, Lord Jesus

p. 23 Let the day end

p. 28 O God of life

p. 36 For all that God can do within us

p. 36 On our hearts and our houses

p. 37 May God watch between you and me

p. 37 May God bless us

p. 37 May God bless us

Wild Goose Publications, Glasgow, *The
Iona Community Worship Book*, 1991:

p. 36 This is the day that the Lord has made

Wild Goose Publications, Glasgow, *The Pattern of our
Days: Liturgies and Resources from the Iona Community*,
edited by Kathy Galloway, 1996:

p. 24 If you come (by Giles David)

p. 24 For loving the world (by Ruth Burgess)

p. 25 God of the past (by Ruth Burgess)

p. 25 In the midst of hunger and war (author unknown)

p. 28 When the world tells us (by Giles David)

p. 31 May God's joy be in your heart (by Joanna
Anderson)

p. 33 Love-giving God (by Ruth Burgess)

p. 34 God, loving *Name* (by Kate Mcllhagga)

p. 35 All our laughter, all our sadness (by Ruth Burgess)

p. 37 In work and worship (author unknown)

p. 38 As you have been fed at this table
(by Kate Mcllhagga)

p. 39 The love of the faithful Creator (by Kate Mcllhagga)

p. 42 Come among us, Jesus (by Ruth Burgess)

p. 43 God of creation, shaper of seas and stars (by
Ruth Burgess)

p. 48 For the greening of the trees (by Kate Mcllhagga)

p. 49 O God, star kindler (by Kate Mcllhagga)

p. 63 I make my circuit (by Kate Mcllhagga)

p. 63 As you were in the ebb and flow (by
Kate Mcllhagga)

p. 65 Bless to us, O God (by Kate Mcllhagga)

introduction

There are many books available already on Celtic Christianity, so why one more? What this resource offers is unique, in that a general overview and taster articles are all included inside one cover. It is intended for:

- *The general enquirer who wants to know just a little about the history and the people of this spirituality.* Shops today offer hundreds of books on general Celtic subjects, often mixing Christian and other approaches. Pagan, Druid, Buddhist, New Age and atheistic authors all nestle together on the shelf. Historical accounts can be rather academic and long. Some authors write on very specific aspects of Celtic spirituality. It can be quite daunting sorting it all out! Here is an overview which will help to find a way through the maze.

- *The activist who wants to begin a journey into the practical implications and applications for everyday life.* Few people live in a hermit's hut by the sea. Most have to relate their inner feelings and desires to the routine of daily work, shopping, driving, and living with neighbours who may or may not be friendly. A religious faith which does not work itself out in the reality of life can be pure escapism. Here are offered fresh insights for seeing an extraordinary God in the ordinary things of life.

- *The soul searching for a way into Celtic insights as an aid to spiritual development.* As life seems to become more computerized, technical, global and impersonal, so the corresponding desire everywhere is not only to maintain but to develop that which makes us human. Love, a sense of purpose, peace and stability, an integrated life, moments of awe and wonder, and an assurance that we are of real value: all these things are at the heart of Celtic spirituality.

- *The church leader who has neither the time nor the money to explore all facets of Celtic Christianity before feeling sufficiently confident to develop worship or give talks on the subject.* The demand for Christian leaders to be aware of religious movements, relate them to social perspectives, and then offer prayerful help is relentless. Church services, school assemblies, home groups, occasional events, are all evaluated ultimately, however, by the vital question: 'Did this help you to meet with the Living God, and what difference has it made to you?' The material contained in these pages has all been tried and tested according to that criterion and contains resources that can form a framework around which occasions for worship can be built. For those who simply want to dip a toe into the water and for those who want to dive in, the possibility is here.

how to use this book

It is impossible to separate the material in this book into disconnected boxes. Like the Celtic knotwork patterns that trace backwards and forwards, over and under, and come back to where they begin, so the contents here are all of a piece, and some repetition is inevitable: for this there is no apology. Different parts of this book can be used in different ways.

For example, in order to *build a service of worship* personal experience shows that a simple skeleton using the material found in these pages works well:

A **hymn** from one of the Iona Wild Goose books.

Play some gentle background **music** for a few minutes as people unwind, then reduce the volume gently as spoken prayers are initiated:

A selection from the **Openings** can be used,

followed by appropriate prayers from **Morning** or **Evening Celebration** prayers which face us with God's glory,

thus leading to **confession**.

This in turn draws us into **thanksgiving** for God's love.

A further **hymn** may be followed by a reading, an anthem, and another **hymn**;

then a sermon expanded from one of the **saints** or **meditation** sections.

Intercessions might then incorporate examples from the **Prayers** section.

A final **hymn** will then be followed by one of the **Celtic blessings**.

Seasonal prayers are included so that particular times of the year can offer specially tailored services. When so many have appreciated the normal round of Celtic services, requests have been made for *baptisms, weddings* and *funerals* in a Celtic style. Consequently, sections of prayers have been included for incorporation at the discretion of the minister. These are meant to be examples only, not an exhaustive list, and what we do not have are authentic ancient services for such events. They simply have not survived. However, since the Celtic tradition is a living river, the answer may be to compose modern prayers in a sympathetic style!

If more than simply a service is envisaged, but rather a whole retreat, quiet day, or awayday, then some of the *activities* could be attempted. Some are clearly more appropriate for adults than children, but that often has more to do with the leader's perception than reality! Obviously it would make sense to explain, for example, the philosophy of the Celtic *knotwork* (from the *Meditation* section), before inviting people to create patterns on *banners* or paper. That way the workshop becomes not just an enjoyable exercise but is lifted into a practical journey of the soul: to create Celtic patterns as an expression of what is going on in our hearts is exactly what the ancient Celtic scribe did. The various sections are specifically designed to fit together like a jigsaw to help people enter into such a total experience.

The very general introductory material on **places to visit** could be brought into a talk on the saint of that place. If a *pilgrimage* is arranged, then clearly the background material on the *saints*, as well as on the place itself, will be useful, and *prayers* and *music* as outlined could all be brought together to give a holistic experience. To pause at any of the places mentioned, gather thoughts quietly, and soak in both the historical information and the atmosphere of the place itself can be quite special. These sites are clearly places made holy and claimed for God. They exist in order to meet with him. What is in these pages can be used to allow the heart and soul to soar in imagination and application as our feet engage with the soil.

In the end, this collection of resources is intended to be simply a taster – an encouraging invitation – to discover more about this fantastic heritage. There is no substitute for the actual doing, creating, travelling, reading, singing and praying. Celtic Christianity is not dead history – it is a living tradition waiting for you to enjoy, breathe in and find your own soul enriched. As that happens so you will find that you too will take things further – further into the past, the present and the future. You will do it with yourself, those around you and with God. Whatever your own spiritual background, tradition or culture, this is not about replacing it with something new: it is about a resource to take you deeper and so be liberated to walk further on your own faith journey.

a celtic revival today?

Any excursion into Celtic spirituality poses two questions for any Christian:

1. What sort of Church do I want to belong to?
2. How does the Church feed my inner soul?

Many today reject the traditional churches because they see not the truth but caricatures loved by the media. These can be painful:

- Autocratic 'Father' can be rejected when portrayed as simply dispensing grace from six feet above contradiction.

- Evangelicals can be dismissed for being more concerned with salvation and doctrinal soundness than with spiritual growth.

- Liberal Christians may be out of favour because having pioneered social activity they are seen to neglect the affairs of the soul.

- Charismatics might be portrayed as often simply desiring any new experience whatever that might be.

- And the institutional churches are viewed as rearranging their structural 'deckchairs' while the Titanic appears to sink! As this goes on many are looking for life-boats elsewhere.

In the meantime, many living in a materialistic but postmodern world feel they are spiritually dying, desperately hungry for soul-food. It is not therefore surprising that they look to the cults, the occult, and a host of New Age philosophies. There is no lack of interest in, or thirst for, contemporary spirituality. Shops sell books by the hundred on spiritual enlightenment. High street stores offer crystals, meditation and relaxation tapes. Community centres host courses for a huge variety of therapies. Horoscopes abound in papers and magazines, and weekend courses on self-realization, stress management and inner healing are there for everyone. It is big business!

Yet only a few seem to go to the churches for a response to these needs. The churches are seen to offer doctrine, rather than spirituality, structures rather than personal growth, and argue endlessly about internal matters while fighting amongst themselves to raise money to maintain their ancient buildings. The problem is that Celtic spirituality can be made to offer whatever people want from it. New Age groups, green activists, feminists, orthodox traditional Christians all claim to be the new Celtic Church. In reality, this 'pick and mix' approach will not do! But in this contemporary desert of hope the reasons for embracing it are clear.

1   A search for our roots

As we become increasingly multi-cultural in society so we welcome the exciting varieties of music, dress and food offered in every high street. But for those who feel insecure the response can be a racist and nationalistic knee-jerk. For others, the response may be a cautious acknowledgement. For some, the acceptance will be enthusiastic. However, a welcoming approach can only really happen from a secure base aware of its own roots. As African, Caribbean, Chinese, Indian, Japanese and other cultures flood in, so for many the knowledge of and pride in our own Celtic roots becomes important. This is important, not as a rebuff to others, but as our own particular contribution into the melting pot of the whole. This becomes especially true as we lose sight of our own family roots through increasing social mobility. It is not surprising that the awakening of Celtic spirituality is happening as a whole industry in tracing family ancestry is booming.

2   A search for historical feminism

Today the contribution and role of women are increasingly recognized, and the dominance of the male is a fact of which many repent. This is true, both in the churches and in society as a whole, where a whole variety of debates continue. Icons from the Celtic churches are held up: Brigid, who according to legend, was consecrated a bishop; Hilda, who ruled over both men and women in her monastery; the references to women deacons in some Celtic churches; the fact that inheritance laws were followed through the maternal line in Druidic societies, and therefore in Celtic tribes and even some churches. While it is in fact quite difficult to argue a coherent feminism from the Celtic churches, supportive traces are most certainly there.

3   A search for the intuitive

It is often said we live in a post-enlightenment age in which philosophical rationalism has had its day. Science has not proved itself as the social saviour, but often is portrayed as the potential destroyer. Theories of chaos now seem to dominate. Economics seem often to serve self-interest, rather than issues of justice, welfare and peace. Education, whether liberal, utilitarian, academic or ideological has often appeared to serve individual progress, rather than that of society as a whole. Even medicine raises ethical questions of terrifying complexity, while increasing numbers look to alternative therapies for the most mundane complaints. In this culture of personal consumerism there is a quest for an inner calm that is to do with the heart, rather than the brain. It is an acceptance that progress (whatever that means) does not necessarily make for a better life. In Celtic spirituality with its accent on the inner promptings of the soul, a willingness to act on dreams and visions, a heart for the poetic and colourful, and an endorsement of the oneness of creation, there can appear to be clues for today.

While these are most certainly there, the danger is of over-romanticism. Amongst everything else must be recalled the harsh disciplines of the Irish penitentials, the disciplines of prayer from standing all night in the North Sea, and the whole strand of the warrior-priest. The Celts were not sloppy thinkers who engaged only gently with life. Intuitive yes, but anaemic no.

Today, people seem to be asking not 'Is it true?' but 'Does it work?' The Celtic churches offer pictures that seem to affirm that it does, but one must be careful in what is being picked out.

4   A search for the green

In an age when we are faced constantly with warnings about the pending ecological disasters of over-population, global warming, food shortages, pollution, Aids, traffic gridlock and industrial chaos, there is always the temptation to look back to a golden age of the garden of Eden. The Celtic era certainly gives a picture of people who had a profound respect for trees, never felling them unless absolutely necessary, and of a people who were aware of the oneness of life – that all species belong to each other and are mutually interdependent. The hundreds of stories of Celtic saints relating with animals, together with the symbolism within Celtic knotwork patterns all testify to this. It is, however, also the case that many Celtic tribes took their enemies' heads as trophies and totems, and tribal warfare was constant. Life was brutal and few were vegetarian until we have the example of leaders like David in his monastery in Wales.

5   A search for a new imagery

Those within Church life have often looked to Taizé, South America or Africa for simple but uplifting music, religious language and experience. In an age of liturgies produced by academic, male, middle-class committees, many are finding the gentle repetitious Celtic prayers very helpful. Not least in this has been the amazing work done by David Adam, Vicar of Lindisfarne, who has discovered a gift for writing modern prayers in an ancient Celtic style. Similarly, from Iona, John Bell and Graham Moule have written earthed liturgies and hymns which underline the incarnational theology of those early Celtic monks. However, they use imagery that confronts and shocks rather than eases us into a selfish and gentle wallowing. This combination of realistic yet glorious imagery being written in these ancient places today is totally consistent with what we know of people like Aidan, Cuthbert and Columba from all those centuries ago. While most certainly not avoiding spiritual truth, it is growth from that truth, rather than simply truth for the sake of conserving doctrinal purity, that is important.

6   A search for autonomy

Curious things are happening around the advent of the Third Millennium. As the Communist bloc breaks up because people cannot belong to the large whole, so local nationalistic temperaments run high. As Britain becomes increasingly centralized, so the call for devolution becomes stronger, interestingly especially from the Celtic countries. As our churches become far more managed, so there is a questioning of the hierarchical structures.

Many are suspicious of institutions, whether political parties or churches. Conversely, many belong to networks and issue groups. There is a willingness to explore and commit oneself to a cause or particular approach, but little inclination to join a traditional group with a wide membership and only vague aims.

Within our churches, the image of loosely associated Celtic monasteries seems attractive when compared to the continental hierarchical model we have largely inherited today. Similarly, the path of an individual working out personal spiritual growth with the aid of a soul-friend seems very attractive when compared simply to receiving impersonal instruction from the pulpit.

The present situation

While the Celtic churches seem to have been systematically destroyed by a combination of the thrust of continental Christianity and the attacks of the Vikings around the coast, there is still in fact a very strong Celtic pull today. Why should half a million people travel to Lindisfarne each year? Humanly it is very difficult to reach. The island itself can only be approached at low tide and it is a very desolate, remote spot. Similarly, why should thousands every year stay on the island of Iona? It takes hours to get there using two ferries and an appalling road across the island of Mull! There is no human reason for these places still to attract people in these numbers, and yet they are seen today as enormously powerful spiritual bases.

In the same way many of our churches today still find themselves very congregational and federal in their attitudes. This rings true with the feel of the Celtic churches who related to each other only as need arose, rather than through some central structure. Everyone today knows just how difficult it is to get Christians to travel from one church to another, rather than attend their own local place of worship on a Sunday. In this country we still tend to be rather anti-authoritarian! For good or ill we are the difficult partner in Europe. We are an island people, and old Celtic customs will not go away.

We need to ask why we still have bonfires in *November*; why each *November* we continue with Remembrance Sunday when so few survivors of the First World War are still with us; why in *November* All Souls' Day and All Saints' Day seem so appropriate. It surely has something to do with the Celtic feel for the cold season of Samhein (November) which was the time of year when the veil drawn between this world and the next seemed very thin. It was the time of year when the weak failed to survive, when thoughts turned to mortality and huddling around the fire became vital. Similarly, we ask why we still insist on celebrating the New Year, which is itself an old Celtic Druid custom.

These things will not go away because they do seem to be part of the flavour of these islands in which we live. So often the Church life we have received, and the teaching which is given, appear to have been imposed from an alien understanding. The genius of the Celtic Christian missionaries was that they worked from within the context of their day. Druid haircuts, monasteries, female leaders, a respect for creation, an intuitive and poetic approach to life, and a great awareness that spirituality is very much greater than Church organization, are all things which continue to ring true today.

It is a fact of life that today the churches which grow tend to be those which are devising their own liturgy, styles of management, and expressions of Christian faith. Just as Christianity in India, Japan and North America will all be quite different, so what happens in the suburbs, the inner city, the new town or the villages of rural England, will by necessity all be quite different. Can we again learn the freedom to express ourselves according to our own culture and context without feeling that we are betraying the wider church? Celtic Christianity is most certainly not another denomination, nor is it an alternative to any existing Christian tradition. It is a challenge for renewal from within – from within the Church, but first from within the heart.

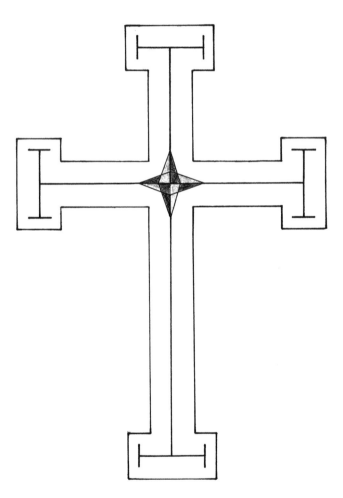

an hístorícal overview

It is very important when we consider Celtic spirituality that we do not live with the impression that it is all about people who sit under a rainbow in the middle of a field having nice green thoughts! The historical context is very important. The heyday for the Celtic churches was about AD 400–900 and in many ways it still lives on in some of the fringes of our islands. However, it is important to remember that there was never any such thing as 'The Celtic Church'. It was never an organized system in the way that we understand churches today. Rather, each Celtic church was highly independent and if there was a relationship between any of them the relationship tended to be one of spiritual support through missionary endeavour, rather than through any particular church structure. It is also important to remember that Celtic church life as it emerged in fifth-century Ireland would be quite different to that which emerged in nineteenth-century Hebridean communities. Even on the mainland the patterns of church life would vary considerably from one place to another, and from one age to another.

Augustine

Generations have been taught that Christianity was brought to this country by St Augustine in AD 597. That is clearly mistaken. The Christian faith had already been here for several centuries. Towards the end of the sixth century a great spiritual leader, Gregory, became Pope. He inherited a Church which was very weak and disorganized. Consequently he set about sending key people throughout the continent to organize this Church, and bring some sense of cohesion. To these islands he sent St Augustine, who came not to convert people, but rather to bring the wayward Celtic churches into line. Then, as now, the life of those in the British Isles tended to be rather separate from the rest of the continent. That small stretch of sea called the English Channel has always acted as something of a barrier, which means that the social, political and religious life of these islands behaves in a rather different way to that on the continent.

There is evidence to suggest that although Augustine baptized many thousands of people, those he did baptise tended to be those who probably were already nominally Christian, rather than those who were new converts. Augustine based himself in Kent and his personal influence was confined to that part of the country. He was allowed to settle there because the king in Kent had married a French princess, so there was already a continental connection, but there was also a realization for those who lived in the affluent south-eastern part of the country that then, as now, its economic future lay in links with the continent.

Soon after his arrival, Augustine decided to meet with the Celtic bishops at Aust, near the River Severn. When the Celtic bishops were summoned they wished to discover whether Augustine, of whom they had never heard, was a true man of God. They consulted with a wise old man who said that it would be his holiness and humility that would mark him out as a true disciple of Jesus. However, when Augustine met these bishops he refused even to rise from his seat. The bishops, affronted by his behaviour, walked out! The relationship between the Celtic and the continental Church could hardly have had a worse start.

Some dates

For those who are historians the evidence of the Christian Church being well rooted here before Augustine is clear:

AD 43 **The Romans occupy Britain**.

cAD 45 **St Paul preaches to the Celts of Galatia**.

AD 70 **Fall of Jerusalem**.

AD 103 Justin Martyr wrote that 'There are Christians in every part of the Roman Empire.'

AD 178 King Lucius, a Christian convert, built a church on what is now the site of St Peter's, Cornhill in London.

AD 190 Tertullian wrote that 'Christianity in Britain has penetrated even those parts the Roman army cannot conquer.'

AD 210 Origen wrote that 'The power of God our Saviour is even with them in Britain.'

AD 303 St Alban was martyred for hiding a Christian priest.

AD 313 **Edict of Milan: Christianity tolerated throughout the Roman Empire**.

AD 314 At the Council of Arles three Celtic bishops attended from York, London and Colchester.

AD 325 **Council of Nicea**.

AD 350 Athanasius wrote about the purity of faith of the British bishops.

AD 375 **Anglo-Saxon settlements begin in Britain**.

AD 400 John Chrysostom wrote that 'There are many churches and altars in Britain'.

AD 410 **Romans leave Britain**.

However, there was a problem. Early Christianity had been imported by the Romans. Consequently the Christian faith was perceived as belonging to an invading army. The only people who had embraced Christianity tended to be Roman soldiers, Roman traders and those wealthy aristocratic families in whose interest it was to do business with their new rulers. This meant that the ordinary, indigenous people would have been very unlikely to have accepted the Christian faith. This in effect means that although Christianity was here early on, it was almost certainly not contextually rooted. The archaeological evidence seems to support this. So when the Romans withdrew from these shores in AD 410 they left behind a vacuum of social, political and religious leadership.

A new wave

Into this void came a variety of people wrestling for power – the Picts, Scots, Saxons and others. Into this void also came a new wave of Christianity. The Roman Christianity had previously been brought across the land, was based on urban centres, and in structure reflected the Roman state system. This new wave of Christianity was brought rather by sea traders who travelled around the coast of the continent. We will all be aware that 'where we are' determines 'who we are'. In other words, our context determines the feel of our society, our personality and our religious faith. Christians in the heart of the East End of London will confront very different issues to those who live in the heart of the countryside. Consequently, the ways in which their faith and worship are expressed will be quite different. So it was for these sea traders who brought their new wave of Christianity. It had within it a feel much more reminiscent of the flow of the tides and the currents, the varieties of weather, the swing of day and night and so on.

This new Christianity appears to have spread like wildfire, first around the coast because that was the way people travelled. Journeying by boat was both safer and swifter than moving across the land. Consequently, all around the coast sprang up small Christian communities, as these Christian traders left something of their faith behind them. The coast was in effect the M25 of its own day (though they probably travelled faster then than we do now!), and the small, simple, isolated monasteries of the coast may have been rather like the motorway service stations, where people stopped for refreshment and renewal along the way.

Synod of Whitby

We could be forgiven for imagining that as the Celtic churches spread their movement from the north, and as Augustine secured his stronghold in the south and began to influence those living further north in the country, that this might appear as a powerful pincer movement on the entire population. However, the Celtic churches had developed in a quite different way from those on the continent. Consequently, when a princess from Kent married a King in Northumbria the two, although Christians, had quite different ways of working-through the practical issues of Christian faith.

In particular, the continental and Celtic churches had different systems for determining the date of Easter, just as today the Eastern Orthodox and Western Churches persist in celebrating Easter on different dates. This came to a head in the Northumbrian court: while one member of this royal couple was *fasting* during the period of Lent, the other was *feasting* to celebrate the Resurrection! A notable person in bringing this to a head was Wilfrid. He had been trained at Lindisfarne, but had travelled extensively on the continent, and was very impressed by what he saw there. It was largely due to his influence that the Synod of Whitby was called in AD 664. This synod was probably the single most significant Church meeting ever to have been held in this country. The three items on the agenda were:

1. To determine the date of Easter for the reasons set out above.

2. To decide whether monks should shave their head according to the continental form of tonsure (symbolising the circular crown of thorns) or, according to the Celtic style (to

shave the front part of the head and allow the back part of the hair to grow into a pony-tail, adopting the form of marking out holy men that was current amongst the Druids of that time).

3.   To determine whether at baptism new converts should be dipped once or thrice in the water.

However, we are all very aware that the items for discussion on an agenda paper bear little resemblance to the real issues underlying the meeting itself!

The continental Church was based on urban centres and organized in a very hierarchical way. The bishop was the ruler of a diocese and the emphasis was very much on unity, power and organization. Apostolic authority was assumed from St Peter, to whom Jesus had given the keys to the kingdom of heaven.

The Celtic churches, on the other hand, were based much more in rural areas, placing them-selves within the tribal societies in which they found themselves. A federal approach was taken with no attempt to govern either from above or from any centre. Rather, each community and church related in a more lateral fashion. In charge of each centre was the abbot, not the bishop. The abbot or abbess was the soul-friend responsible for all in the monastery, and *under* him or her would have been a bishop. The bishop's task was to ordain and to evangelize. The Celtic churches were materially very poor. They took their authority from St John, the 'beloved disciple' of Jesus, the disciple of love.

At this great synod, Cedd was chosen to be the interpreter between the two sides, partly because he could speak both Latin and Irish, but also because both sides felt he was somebody they could each trust. At the end of the day it was the continental approach that was adopted because it was argued that if St Peter had been given the keys to the kingdom of heaven by Jesus, nobody dare argue with that!

It is a moot point whether or not it was a foregone conclusion. Those who argued for the con-tinental approach were much better experienced in rhetoric and argument, and had a much more coherent presentation than the Celtic representatives who relied much more on intu-ition, and probably seemed quite rustic by comparison. Once the decision had been taken that the Church should be organized according to the continental system, many of the Celtic lead-ers retreated north to Scotland, and subsequently to Ireland, in dismay. At the same time Viking raids were increasing around the coast, and because many of the monasteries were coastal it meant they were easy prey. The Celtic centres therefore became increasingly deserted and defeated, and decreased as places of influence.

Today

As with any battle, it is the victors who write the history in their own terms. Consequently, when we read Bede (our major historical source), although in many ways he is sympathetic to the cause of the Celtic churches, he makes his feelings quite clear. His thesis, as he looked out over a later Church which was becoming rather lax and corrupt, is that while the Celtic churches were very moral and very spiritual, they were also perhaps rather simple. What was needed, he argues, was the strategy, coherence, and disciplined mind of the continental

Church. His argument, therefore, is that both Celtic and continental needed each other. It is, in fact, difficult to know whether the Celtic churches would have survived without the strength of a continental pattern of organization

The issue remains, however. For many today who wish to explore the Christian faith, the institutional church is a real problem while an intuitive approach to spirituality proves amazingly attractive. The task today, as then, is to maintain a Christian spirituality within our own context, and to organize ourselves in a way that is humanly helpful, without the demands of the system totally overpowering the very thing for which the Christian faith stands. The Synod of Whitby may have taken place historically many centuries ago, but in reality it is re-enacted in every generation, in every place, and in the life of every spiritually searching human being.

liturgies

introduction

The prayers in this section are taken from a variety of sources, both ancient and contemporary. This is quite deliberate as the Celtic tradition is a living stream of faith, not something fixed in the past. Some were originally intended for individual use and others for corporate use. You may care to consider how to break any of the prayers so that some lines are said by a leader and some by the congregation. Those written originally with this in mind are differentiated with the congregational words in italics. They are offered as examples, not as an exhaustive collection. Readers may wish to adapt other Celtic prayers in this way, or, best of all, to create new ones in this style.

As with all the prayers offered here, they should always be said gently and slowly but with clarity and a sense of life, giving people time to consider the imagery and to feel that the pace of praying accords with their own heartbeat.

One way of putting a simple service together is outlined in the section above, *How to use this book*. It is always important to remember that a service of worship is not a concert, nor just a human arrangement of material. Offer your planning to God first. Offer your imagination so that when you come to visualize it, nothing is forgotten: the appropriate level of lighting, the arrangement of seats, any visual focus, where musicians might be, the level of sound required, and so on. It is about creating the right conditions for people to feel their souls can relax and hearts open up in an environment in which it feels safe to acknowledge challenge. Finally, the assessment is not made according to how many people say, 'That was nice', but rather how many indicate that they have engaged with the living God.

openings

Lord, stretch out towards those who cannot pray:
those for whom prayer is merely a routine,
those who use prayer as a substitute for action,
those who are proud of their prayers,
those whose prayers do not carry over into daily life,
those who feel no-one prays for them,
those who feel they have no-one to pray to.

Church of Scotland

May Sunday be a day of resurrection;
a day of refreshment for families
and single people,
for traders and communities.
May our homes be places of hospitality and hope,
that we may know your risen presence
as we share lives
and enjoy the company of others.
May our churches worship in a way
that brings honour to you,
joy to the people,
and healing to the land.

Ray Simpson

Bright shining star,
blessed be each thing
your eye lights on.
Radiant summer sun,
blessed be each thing
your smile touches.
As night and day
you warm and bless us,
so one day
shall the Lord, your creator
be our everlasting Light.

Son of God,
work in me
and through me
that I may shine
like the stars.
Shine through me
that I may reflect
your glorious light,

and sharing a sense of wonder
may point the way to God.

Spirit of God,
coax me from my hiding place.
Draw me out
to witness to God's love.
Restore my zest for life
that all that I do
may be to your glory.

Kate McIlhagga

As the tide draws the waters
close in upon the shore
Make me an island,
set apart,
Alone with you, God,
Holy to you.

Then with the turning of the tide
Prepare me to carry your presence
to the busy world beyond,
the world that rushes in on me
Till the water come again
and fold me back to you.

Andy Rayne, from The Aidan Office, Celtic Night Prayer

I am bending my knee
In the eye of the Father who created me,
In the eye of the Son who died for me,
In the eye of the Spirit who cleansed me,
In love and desire.

Pour down upon us from heaven
The rich blessing of Thy forgiveness;
Thou who art uppermost in the City,
Be Thou patient with us.

Grant to us, Thou Saviour of Glory,
The fear of God, the love of God, and His affection,
And the will of God to do on earth at all times
As angels and saints do in heaven;
Each day and night give us Thy peace.
Each day and night give us Thy peace.

Adapted from Carmina Gadelica

morning

O God, you summon the day to dawn,
You teach the morning to waken the earth.
Great is your name.
Great is your love.
For you the valleys shall sing for joy,
The trees of the field shall clap their hands.
Great is your name.
Great is your love.
For you the kings of the earth shall bow,
The poor and persecuted shall shout for joy.
Great is your name.
Great is your love.
Your love and mercy shall last forever,
Fresh as the morning, sure as the sunrise.
Great is your name.
Great is your love.

Wild Goose Resource Group

Bless to me, O God,
Each thing mine eye sees;
Bless to me, O God,
Each sound mine ear hears;
Bless to me, O God,
Each odour that goes to my nostrils;
Bless to me, O God,
Each taste that goes to my lips,
Each note that goes to my song,
Each ray that guides my way,
Each thing that I pursue,
Each lure that tempts my will,
The zeal that seeks my living soul,
The Three that seek my heart,
The zeal that seeks my living soul,
The Three that seek my heart.

Adapted from *Carmina Gadelica*

God of the dawning,
Christ of the sea,
Spirit, giver of breath to me,
Trinity blessed, all praise to thee,
Giving this day of newness to me.

Bless me today body and soul,
Bless me today and keep me whole,
Bless me today in all that I do,
Bless my powers, they come from you.

David Adam

O Lord of all creation,
you were with me from my very beginning.
You knew me before my parents did.
I have no memory of my birth,
but you knew me,
and loved me from the moment of my conception.
Help me not to forget that you are with me
and for me at all new beginnings;
each new day,
each fresh challenge,
each new joy or sorrow.
I need fear nothing.
You are always there.

Church of Scotland

Thanks to you, O God, that I have risen today,
To the rising of this life itself;
May it be to your own glory,
O God of every gift,
And to the glory of my soul likewise.
O great God, aid my soul
With the aiding of your own mercy;
Even as I clothe my body with wool,
Cover my soul with the shadow of your wing.
Help me to avoid every sin,
And the source of every sin to forsake;
And as the mist scatters
on the crest of the hills,
May each ill haze clear from my soul, O God.

Adapted from Carmina Gadelica

Thanks be to you, O God,
That we have risen this day.
Thanks be to you O God,
For our coming in safety to this place.
Be the purpose of God between us and each purpose.
The hand of God between us and each hand.
Be the pain of Christ between us and each pain,
The love of Christ between us and each love.

Kate McIlhagga

evening

Come, Lord Jesus,
You too were tired
When day was done;
You met your friends at evening time.
Come, Lord Jesus.

Come, Lord Jesus,
You too enjoyed
When nights drew on;
You told your tales at close of day.
Come, Lord Jesus.

Come, Lord Jesus.
You kindled faith
When lamps were low;
You opened scriptures,
broke the bread
and shed your light
As darkness fell.
Come, Lord Jesus,
And meet us here.

Wild Goose Resource Group

Leader	Shadows lengthen,
A	darkness thickens,
B	the lights are lit,
All	*and the day we have lived through*
	comes to an end.

Leader	Let us worship the God
	who separated light from darkness.
All	*Hallowed be his name.*

Leader	Let us worship the God
	who ordered the birth of the stars.
All	*Hallowed be his name.*

Leader	Who watches over us, unsleeping,
	night and day.
All	*Hallowed be his name.*

Susan Sayers

Let the day end,
the night fall,
the world move into silence,
And let God's people say Amen.
Amen.

Let minds unwind,
hearts be still,
bodies relax,
And let God's people say Amen.
Amen.

But before the day is done,
Let God's holy name be praised,
And let God's people say Amen.
Amen.

Wild Goose Resource Group

Leader	Through our nights and days,
A	through our sleeping and waking,
B	through our resting and working,
All	*keep us mindful of your presence, holy God.*

Leader	Through places of darkness,
A	when we cannot see,
B	when we stumble,
All	*keep us mindful of your faithful love.*

Leader	When evil threatens,
A	deceiving and unnerving us,
B	masquerading as light,
All	*keep us mindful of your strong protection.*

Leader	We call to mind those whose shift is just beginning; those who are dreading this night;
All	*Lord, have mercy.*

Leader	We call to mind those who will have no shelter or adequate accommodation; those for whom the comfort of sleep does not come and whose minds cannot rest;
All	*Lord, have mercy.*

Susan Sayers

thanksgiving

If you come
in certainty or in confusion
in anger or in anguish
This time is for us.

If you come
in silent suffering or hidden sorrow
in pain or promise
This time is for us.

If you come
for your own or another's need
for a private wound or the wound of the world
This time is for us.

If you come
and do not know why
to be here is enough
This time is for us all.

Come now, Christ of the forgiving warmth
Come now, Christ of the yearning tears
Come now, Christ of the transforming touch
This time is for you.

Giles David, from *The Pattern of our Days*

For loving the world and knowing our names
thank you God
Thank you God.

For your strength that fills us
and your love that heals us
thank you God
Thank you God.

For your presence here with us today
and for your hand that leads us into tomorrow
thank you God
Thank you God.

Come bless us, hold us, wrestle with us,
warm us in your embrace
For we are your people
And you are our justice and joy.
Amen.

Ruth Burgess, from *The Pattern of our Days*

God of the past who has fathered and mothered us
We are here to thank you.

God of the future who is always ahead of us
We are here to trust you.

God of the present here in the midst of us
We are here to praise you.

God of life beyond us within us
We rejoice in your glorious love.

Ruth Burgess, from *The Pattern of our Days*

In the midst of hunger and war
We celebrate the promise
Of peace and plenty.
In the midst of oppression and tyranny
We celebrate the promise
Of service and freedom.
In the midst of doubt and despair
We celebrate the promise
Of faith and hope.
In the midst of fear and betrayal
We celebrate the promise
Of joy and loyalty.
In the midst of hatred and death
We celebrate the promise
Of love and life.
In the midst of sin and decay
We celebrate the promise
Of salvation and renewal.
In the midst of death on every side
We celebrate the promise
Of the loving Christ.

Author unknown, from *The Pattern of our Days*

celebration

There are times when I feel happy:
just being with friends can make me laugh in pure joy;
thank you, God, for the blessing of shared laughter.
It is your gift too that I can laugh at myself,
at my quaint and quirky ways,
at the daft things I say and do.

Thank you, God,
for those who are the life and soul of the party,
for those whose sense of humour is infectious,
for those who are just a good laugh,
for laughter's cleansing power.

Thank you, God,
for laughing at us,
for poking fun at our pomposity,
bursting the balloon of the unco guid.*

Lord,
you give us the gift of laughter;
help us to share our laughter with others,
to lighten their lives as well as our own.

*unco guid – pride
Church of Scotland

The glory of God in my working.
The glory of God in my speaking.
The glory of God in my eating.
The glory of God in my resting.
The glory of God in my thinking.
The glory of God in my looking.
The glory of God in my listening.
The glory of God in my travelling.
The glory of God in my crying.
The glory of God in my loving
The glory of God in the present moment.

Ray Simpson

I believe, O God of all gods,
That you are the eternal Creator of life.
I believe, O God of all gods,
That you are the eternal Father of love.
I believe, O Lord and God of the peoples,
That you are the Creator of the high heavens.
I believe, O Lord and God of the peoples,
That you created my soul and set its warp.

Carmina Gadelica

Leader	Wherever you call us, Lord, our God,
All	*we want to be ready and willing to go.*
Leader	Whenever you need us, Lord, our God,
All	*we want to be available and attentive.*
Leader	Whoever turns out to be our neighbour in need,
All	*we want to be happy to serve, without exceptions.*
Leader	Live within us, Lord our God,
All	*so that we notice with your discernment,*
	respond with your compassion,
	and speak with your integrity.
	In our lives and in our world,
	let your kingdom come.
	Amen.

Susan Sayers

confession

When the world tells us
we are what we do with
our activity, acumen or achievement
let us learn
We are what we do with our silence.

When the world tells us
we are what we do with
our spending power, selling power,
or our power of speech
let us learn
We are what we do with our silence.

When the world tells us
to drown the silent sufferings of others
with indifference or noise
or to forget the art of stillness even in the storm
let us learn
We are what we do with our silence.

Where the world tells us
to rush in where angels fear to tread
let us learn that angels listen first
before they take a step
for the voice of God in the silence . . .

Silence

Giles David, from *The Pattern of our Days*

O God of life,
Eternity cannot hold you,
Nor can our little words catch
The magnificence of your kindness,
Yet in the space of our small hearts
And in silence
You can come close and repair us.

silence

O God of life,
Grant us your forgiveness
For our wild thoughts.
For our wild deeds,
For our empty speech
And the words with which we wounded.

silence

O God of life,
Grant us your forgiveness,
For our false desires,
For our hateful actions,
For our wastefulness,
And for all we left unattended.

silence

O Loving Christ,
Hanged on a tree
Yet risen in the morning,
Scatter the sin from our souls
As the mist from the hills;
Begin what we do,
Inform what we say,
Redeem who we are.

In you we place our hope,
Our great hope,
Our living hope,
This day and evermore.
Amen.

Wild Goose Resource Group

Lord,
Let our memory
provide no shelter
for grievance against another.

Lord,
Let our heart
provide no harbour
for hatred of another.

Lord,
Let our tongue
be no accomplice
in the judgement of a brother.

from The Cuthbert Office, *Celtic Night Prayer*

The Father is always present.
Forgive us for not reflecting your faithfulness.
The Son is always self-giving.
Forgive us for living for ourselves.
The Spirit always leads us on.
Forgive us for holding back.

Ray Simpson

Baptisms

In name of God,
In name of Jesus,
In name of Spirit,
The perfect Three of power.

The little drop of the Father
On your little forehead, beloved one.

The little drop of the Son
On your little forehead, beloved one.

The little drop of the Spirit
On your little forehead, beloved one.

To aid you, to guard you,
To shield you, to surround you.

To keep you from the spirits,
To shield you from the host.

To save you from the gnome,
To deliver you from the spectre.

The little drop of the Three
To shield you from the sorrow.

The little drop of the Three
To fill you with Their pleasantness.

The little drop of the Three
To fill you with Their virtue.

O the little drop of the Three
To fill you with Their virtue.

Carmina Gadelica

A wavelet for your form,
A wavelet for your voice,
A wavelet for your sweet speech;

A wavelet for your luck,
A wavelet for your good,
A wavelet for your health;

A wavelet for your throat,
A wavelet for your pluck,
A wavelet for your graciousness;
Nine waves for your graciousness.

Carmina Gadelica

May God's joy be in your heart
and God's love surround your living.
Each day and night
and wherever you roam.
May you know God's presence.
In growing and learning,
in joy and sorrow,
in friendship,
in solitude,
in beginnings and endings.
May God keep you and bless you
all the days of your life.

Joanna Anderson, from *The Pattern of our Days*

A small drop of water
To your forehead, beloved,
Meet for Father, Son and Spirit,
The Triune of power.

A small drop of water
To encompass my beloved,
Meet for Father, Son and Spirit,
The Triune of power.

A small drop of water
To fill you with each grace,
Meet for Father, Son and Spirit,
The Triune of power.

Carmina Gadelica

marriages

Peace in your thinking. Peace in your hearts.
Peace with creation. Peace with one another.
The peace of Christ be with you.
The peace of Christ be with you.

Ray Simpson

Lord, today brings
Paths to discover
Possibilities to choose
People to encounter
Peace to possess
Promises to fulfil
Perplexities to ponder
Power to strengthen
Pointers to guide
Pardon to accept
Praises to sing
and a Presence to proclaim.

David Adam

God bless your house
From roof to floor,
From ground to sky,
From wall to wall,
From end to end,
From its foundations
And in its covering.

The Brigid Office, *Celtic Night Prayer*,
loosely based on a prayer from *Carmina Gadelica*

Come Lord, come light, come love.
Come down,
Come in,
Come among us.
Come Presence, come peace, come power.
Come down,
Come in,
Come among us.
Come Grace, come glory, come goodness.

Come down,
Come in,
Come among us.
Come Creator, come Redeemer, come Strengthener,
Come down,
Come in,
Come among us.
Come Father, come Son, come Spirit,
Come down,
Come in,
Come among us.

David Adam

Love-giving God
who created us in your image
who walked with us in a garden
heard our laughter, our quarrels
promised us heirs and a community of hope
God who brought us forth
nurtured and fed us
taught us to walk and run and grow
made us for each other,
let your love surround and lead
Name and *Name* today and always.

Love-making Christ
Carpenter, Teacher, Friend,
who changed water into wine at weddings
cracked jokes about camels
and took upon yourself the heavy yoke
of the world's sins:
Christ alive – in our lives
in our community
in our world
let your love embrace and reconcile
Name and *Name* today and always.

Loving Spirit
whose breath soft as butterfly wings
can move mountains
whose fire can cleanse and renew;
Spirit vibrant with joy and peace
let your love comfort and challenge
Name and *Name* today and always.

Ruth Burgess, from *The Pattern of our Days*

funerals

God, loving *Name*
nearer to us than our next breath
be with those who mourn.
Be in their shock, their grief,
their anger and despair
that they may grieve,
but not as those without hope.

Forgive all the harm they/we feel
they/we have done to *Name*
and show them/us that they/we are forgiven.

We offer to you
all the regrets
the memories
the pain
the 'if only'
knowing that you
will surround those we mourn
with your presence,
and heal them and us
of all that harms us.

Kate McIlhagga, from The Pattern of our Days

Into the darkness and warmth of the earth
We lay you down.

Into the sadness and smiles of our memories
We lay you down.

Into the cycle of living and dying and rising again
We lay you down.

May you rest in peace, in fulfilment, in loving
May you run straight home
Into God's embrace.

Ruth Burgess, from Book of a Thousand Prayers

Go forth upon your journey from this world,
In the Name of God the father who created you;
In the Name of Jesus Christ who died for you;
In the Name of the Holy Spirit
who shines through you;
In friendship with God's saints;
Aided by the holy angels.
May you rest this day
In the peace and love
Of your eternal home.

Traditional (adapted)

I am going home with You, to your home, to your home;
I am going home with You, to your home of mercy;
I am going home with You, to your home, to your home;
I am going home with You, to the Fount of all the blessings.

Carmina Gadelica

In the name of the all powerful Father,
In the name of the all loving Son,
In the name of the all pervading Spirit.
I command all spirit of fear to leave you,
I break the power of unforgiven sin in you,
I set you free from dependence upon human ties
That you may be as free as the wind,
As soft as sheep's wool,
As straight as an arrow;
And that you may journey into the Heart of God.

Community of Aidan and Hilda

All our laughter, all our sadness
Safe now in God's hands

All our anger, all our gladness
Safe now in God's hands

All our stories, all our memories
Safe now in God's hands

Those we remember, those we love
Safe now in God's hands.

Ruth Burgess, from *The Pattern of our Days*

endings

For all that God can do within us,
For all that God can do without us,
Thanks be to God.

For all in whom Christ lived before us,
For all in whom Christ lives beside us,
Thanks be to God.

For all the Spirit wants to bring us,
For where the Spirit wants to send us,
Thanks be to God.

Listen.
Christ has promised to be with us in the world as in our
worship.
Amen. We go to meet him.

Wild Goose Resource Group

On our hearts and our houses,
The blessing of God.
In our coming and going,
The peace of God.
In our life and believing,
The love of God.
At our end and new beginning,
The arms of God
To welcome us
And bring us home. Amen.

Wild Goose Resource Group

This is the day that the Lord has made.
We will rejoice and be glad in it.
We will not offer to God
Offerings that cost us nothing.
Go in peace and serve the Lord.
We will seek peace and pursue it.
Glory be to the Creator to the Son,
and to the Holy Spirit,
As it was in the beginning
Is now and shall be for ever. Amen.

Wild Goose Publications

May God watch between you and me,
While we are parted, one from another.
May Christ stay beside you and me,
While we are parted, one from another.
And in the shadow of the Spirit's wing,
May we pass this night in peace. Amen.

Wild Goose Resource Group

May God bless us;
May God keep us in the Spirit's care
And lead our lives with love.

May God's warm welcome shine from our hearts,
And Christ's own peace prevail
Through this and every day
Till greater life shall call. Amen.

Wild Goose Resource Group

May the peace of the Lord Christ go with you,
wherever He may send you,
May He guide you
through the wilderness,
protect you
through the storm.
May He bring you home rejoicing
at the wonders He has shown you.
May He bring you home rejoicing
once again into our doors.

Peter Sutcliffe, from Morning Office,
Celtic Daily Prayer

May God bless us
In our sleep with rest,
In our dreams with vision,
In our waking with a calm mind,
In our souls with the friendship of the Holy Spirit
This night and every night. Amen.

Wild Goose Resource Group

In work and worship
God is with us.
Gathered and scattered
God is with us.
Now and always
God is with us.
Amen.

From *The Pattern of our Days*

Blessings 1

May the eye of the great God
The eye of the God of glory,
The eye of the Virgin's Son,
The eye of the gentle Spirit
Aid you and shepherd you
In every time,
Pour upon you every hour
Mild and generously.

Carmina Gadelica

Gentle peace . . .
Flows freely
Encircles fully
Refreshes gently
Comforts warmly
Reassures softly
Forgives easily
Fulfils entirely
Gentle peace . . .

Amelia Beane

God's grace distil on you,
Christ's grace distil on you,
Spirit's grace distil on you
Each day and each night
Of your portion in the world;
On each day and each night
Of your portion in the world.

Carmina Gadelica

As you have been fed at this table
go to feed the hungry.
As you have been set free
go to set free the imprisoned.
As you have received, give:
as you have heard, proclaim.
And the blessing which you have received
from Father, Son and Holy Spirit
be always with you.

Kate McIlhagga, from *The Pattern of our Days*

The love and affection of the angels be to you,
The love and affection of the saints be to you,
The love and affection of heaven be to you,
To guard you and to cherish you.

May God shield you on every steep,
May Christ aid you on every path,
May Spirit fill you on every slope,
On hill and on plain.

Carmina Gadelica

The love of the faithful Creator
The peace of the wounded Healer
The joy of the challenging Spirit
The hope of the Three in One
surround and encourage you
today, tonight and forever.

Kate McIlhagga, from *The Pattern of our Days*

Blessings 2

Deep peace of the running wave to you
Deep peace of the flowing air to you
Deep peace of the quiet earth to you
Deep peace of the shining stars to you
Deep peace of the Son of peace to you.

Traditional Scottish

The guarding of the God of life be upon me,
The guarding of loving Christ be upon me,
The guarding of the Holy Spirit be upon me,
Each step of the way,
To aid me and enfold me,
Each day and night of my life.

Carmina Gadelica

The sacred Three
To save,
To shield,
To surround
The hearth,
The house,
The household,
This eve,
This night, oh!
This eve,
This night,
And every night,
Each single night.

Carmina Gadelica

With these hands I bless the lonely,
the forgotten and the lost;
With these hands I shield you messengers
from attacks within, without;
With these hands I dispel darkness
and rebuke evil forces;
With these hands I pray your victory
for fighting ones and dying.

Community of Aidan and Hilda

May the eyes of the Creator behold you,
May the hands of the Saviour uphold you,
May the arms of the Spirit enfold you.

Traditional Irish

May the road rise to meet you
May the wind be always at your back
May the sun shine warm upon your face
The rain fall soft upon your fields
And until we meet again
May God hold you
In the hollow of his hand.

Traditional Irish

The blessing-help of the Three upon my wishing,
The blessing-help of the Three upon my willing,
The blessing-help of the Three upon my walking,
And upon my knees that they may never weaken.

Traditional Irish

christmas

Come among us, Jesus
You whom the angels worship
and children welcome
Come Jesus, and meet us here.

Come among us, Jesus
You who hurled the stars into space
and shaped the spider's weaving
Come Jesus, and meet us here.

Come among us, Jesus
You who walked the long road to Bethlehem
and lit a flame that dances forever
Come Jesus, and meet us here.

Ruth Burgess, from *The Pattern of our Days*

Jesus, born a refugee,
Come among us.
Jesus, friend of the poor,
Come among us.
Jesus, lover of the outcast,
Come among us.
Christ, food for the hungry,
Come among us.
Christ, health of the sick,
Come among us.
Christ, saviour of the world,
Come among us.
Jesus, bringer of good news,
Come among us.
Jesus, hope of us all,
Come among us.

David Adam

I open the stable door,
I kneel before the infant.
I worship with the shepherds.
I adore the Christ child.
I ponder the Word made flesh.
I absorb the love of God.
I sing Glory with the Angels.
I offer my gifts with the Magi.
I have come from lands afar.
I receive the living Lord.
I hold him in my hands.
I go on my way rejoicing,
Glorifying and praising God.

David Adam

God of creation, shaper of seas and stars
of planets and of people
God is here with us.

God, born in Bethlehem
gurgling, crying, laid in a manger
God is here with us.

God, breath of the universe
flickering, dancing in the candle flame
God is here with us.

God, Immanuel, amongst us, within us
We bring ourselves and our dreams,
For we want to be here with you.

Ruth Burgess, from *The Pattern of our Days*

Dear Son of Mary, change my heart;
You took flesh to redeem me;
Forgive my backsliding;
Dear Son of God, change my heart.

Dear Son of God, take my heart;
You suffered for me;
Forgive my waywardness;
Dear Son of Mary, take my heart.

Eighth century

easter

O King of the Friday
Whose limbs were stretched on the cross,
O Lord who did suffer
The bruises, the wounds, the loss.
We stretch ourselves beneath the shield of your might;
Some fruit from the tree of your passion
Fall on us this night!

Traditional Irish

The Lord of the empty tomb
The conqueror of gloom
Come to you

The Lord in the garden walking
The Lord to Mary talking
Come to you

The Lord in the Upper Room
Dispelling fear and doom
Come to you

The Lord on the road to Emmaus
The Lord giving hope to Thomas
Come to you

The Lord appearing on the shore
Giving us life for evermore
Come to you

David Adam

By your death upon the cross
Raise us, good Lord.
By your burial in the grave
Raise us, good Lord.
By your descending into hell
Raise us, good Lord.
By your mighty resurrection
Raise us, good Lord.

By your conquering death
Raise us, good Lord.

By your risen appearances
Raise us, good Lord.
By your presence among us
Raise us, good Lord.

David Adam

The Cross of Christ
Upon your brow
The Cross of Christ
Protect you now

The Cross of Christ
Upon your mind
The Cross of Christ
Make you kind

The Cross of Christ
Upon your head
The Cross of Christ
Save from dread

The Cross of Christ
Upon your face
The Cross of Christ
Give you grace

The Cross of Christ
Upon your heart
The Cross of Christ
Set you apart

The Cross of Christ
Upon your soul
The Cross of Christ
Keep you whole

David Adam

We offer You:
Our tears
The spice of our faith
The ointment of our tenderness
The flowers of our personality
Memories of our meeting
Of words of eternal life
Our gentle touch.

Community of Aidan and Hilda

pentecost

Creator Spirit, come,
Renew the face of the earth.
Kindling Spirit, come,
Inflame our waiting hearts.
Anointing Spirit, come,
Pour forth on us anew.

You led your people by a cloud
May your Spirit lead us all today
You led your people by fire at night
May your Spirit lighten up our way
Wind of God, blow us to wild places as You will
Breeze of God, refresh us as you desire
Breath of God, blow away all that is unclean
Rain of God, revive our withered lives
River of God, flow through us and heal our land
River of God, flow through us and heal our land.

Community of Aidan and Hilda

Spirit of God
The breath of creation is yours.

Spirit of God
The groans of the world are yours.

Spirit of God
The wonder of communion is yours.

Spirit of God
The fire of love is yours.

And we are filled
And we are filled.

Community of Aidan and Hilda

When I feel alone
Your Presence is ever with me.
Come Holy Dove
Cover with love.

When I am in the dark
Your light is all around me.
Come Holy Dove
Cover with love.

When I am in the cold
Your warmth will enfold me.
Come Holy Dove
Cover with love.

When I feel weak
Your strength will seek me.
Come Holy Dove
Cover with love.

When I am sad
Your joy will make me glad.
Come Holy Dove
Cover with love.

When I am sick and ill
Your health will heal me still.
Come Holy Dove
Cover with love.

Spirit be about my head
Spirit peace around me shed
Spirit light about my way
Spirit guardian night and day.

Come Holy Dove
Cover with love.

David Adam

harvest

You are the Maker
Of earth and sky,
You are the Maker
Of heaven on high.
You are the Maker
Of oceans deep,
You are the Maker
Of mountains steep.
You are the Maker
Of sun and rain,
You are the Maker
Of hill and plain.
You are the Maker
Of such as me.
Keep me, O Lord,
Eternally.

David Adam

For the greening of trees
and the gentling of friends
we thank you, O God.

For the brightness of field
and the warmth of the sun
we thank you, O God.

For work to be done
and laughter to share
we thank you, O God.

We thank you, and know
that through struggle and pain
in the slippery path of new birth
hope will be born
and all shall be well.

Kate McIllhagga, from *The Pattern of our Days*

Bless, O God, my little cow,
Bless, O God, my desire;
Bless Thou my partnership
And the milking of my hand, O God.

Bless, O God, each teat,
Bless, O God, each finger;
Bless Thou each drop
That goes into my pitcher, O God!

Carmina Gadelica

Where the mist rises from the sea,
Where the waves creep upon the shore,
Where the wrack lifts upon the strand,
I have seen the Lord.

Where the sun awakens the day,
Where the road winds on its way,
Where the fields are sweet with hay,
I have seen the Lord.

Where the stars shine in the sky,
Where the streets so peaceful lie,
Where the darkness is so nigh,
I have seen the Lord.

David Adam

O God, star kindler
kindle a flame of love within us
to light our path in days of darkness

O God, sun warmer
warm us with your love
to melt the frozen hand of guilt

O God, moon burnisher
burnish the shield of faith
that we may seek justice
and follow the ways of peace.

Kate McIlhagga

music resources in worship

There are two difficulties here: the first is that musical appreciation is a very subjective matter and Christians, like others, divide very deeply over what they like and dislike; the second is that, riding on the crest of the current wave of interest in Celtic matters, it is the habit of music producers to label a CD or tape 'Celtic' in the hope of selling more!

It does seem a fact, however, that people appreciate the opportunity to be quiet and so get in touch with their inner selves and with God. This often happens most easily in an atmosphere of controlled peace. Personal experience has shown that a combination of thoughtful Celtic liturgy and gentle Irish or Scottish music enables just this. Among the best thoughtful and thought-provoking liturgy is that from the Wild Goose books produced by the Iona Community. Here are prayers and meditations not to be hurried, but to be led in a very quiet, gentle, slow and meditative way.

These can be greatly enhanced by the use of music: if no resident musician is available then recorded tapes or CDs are fine. People are invited to relax and simply let the issues of the day float away: to close their eyes and let the music and words carry them along. Play one whole track (a full three minutes) from any of the sources mentioned below, and then also play music quietly 'underneath' the spoken prayers, increasing the volume slightly between each prayer or short section of liturgy, say for one minute at a time. Then at the end of the prayers continue with the music for a full further three minutes. Quiet, space, a sense of ease, and the freedom just to be and meditate is amazingly valuable.

Annie Mawson from the Lake District plays the Celtic harps superbly for such occasions nationwide, and has produced several CDs including *If you stand very still*, a collection of instrumental pieces which are most apt.

The author has compiled his own tapes using the gentler pipe or harp music from sources such as *Visions of Ireland* by Michael and Eilish, the *Skylark* series by Hilary Rushmer, *Celtic Harp* series by Patrick Ball, and *Harpbreakers* by Sileas. These are all available from good music stores, and Navada record label produces a lot of Celtic material. Any music by the eighteenth-century Irish harpist O'Carolan is excellent in this context, and it is worth remembering that the gentler music of artists like Enya should not be overlooked.

The Iona Community has recorded much of its own musical material, and this will help others to understand how such songs and hymns might sound, while Sammy Horner (*Celtic Praise 1, 2* and *3*) records a very earthy style of both song and music.

A useful list is included at the end of this book.

hymns and songs

There are several approaches that may be appropriate for including songs in any time of praise and worship with a Celtic feel.

1. Some words are available which can trace their roots back to particular Celtic saints. The most obvious might be 'Be thou my vision' drawing on St Patrick's Breastplate, together with 'Christ be beside me, Christ be before me' (tune: 'Bunessan'). Looking through the index of any hymn book will reveal such hymns. Poems do exist which are attributed to Columba and Caedmon, but whether these can successfully be adapted and set to music has yet to be seen.

2. The most obvious source of modern material is from the Wild Goose Worship Group of the Iona Community. John Bell and Graham Moule in particular have composed hymns not only about particular saints and Celtic themes, but have also written words that are amazingly challenging and confront the mind as well as the heart. 'Oh where are you going', 'Will you come and follow me', 'How can we live as Christians here', 'Jesus Christ is waiting', and 'Inspired by love and anger' have already found their way into many hymn books. Here we are presented with a clear incarnational theology which matches the glorious imagery of their prayer material.

3. There will be others who will feel comfortable with songs that can be sung to Celtic tunes. Examples include 'I cannot tell' (tune: 'Londonderry Air') and 'Spirit of God unseen as the wind' (tune: 'Skye Boat Song'). There are many others.

4. Others will wish to explore further. The Celtic missionaries were always keen to work within the culture they entered. In these Celtic islands there is a fund of traditional folk music which resides (often buried deep) in the memories of many of the population. It is therefore a thoroughly Celtic approach, for example, to sing 'We worship God in harmony' (tune: 'Auld Lang Syne') and 'My Lord of light' (tune: 'Barbara Allen') or to use international folk tunes such as 'Kumbayah' for a setting of the Lord's Prayer, to sing 'What a friend we have in Jesus' to the tune of 'The carnival is over', and 'Spirit of holiness' to the tune of 'Blow the wind southerly'.

5. Ultimately, of course, the challenge is to compose new meaningful words to tunes currently accepted as having contemporary cultural significance. To compose such words employing realistic theology, practice and understanding from the insights of Celtic Christianity will be a major contribution in rooting the Christian faith in today's society. Workshops run for groups of Christians inviting them to do this can be most revealing!

prayers

introduction

The prayers in this section, again from a variety of sources and centuries, are offered as starting points. They may be used as prayers standing in their own right, or as focus points when the intercessions are being led in a service of worship. Personal and more extemporary prayers then become anchored within a considered and poetic framework. This can help to keep a shape that is easier to follow, and can balance language that may not always have been thought through quite as carefully.

Alternatively, these are prayers which may be inserted quite deliberately at the end of each section in a sermon. If a sermon or talk begins with a gentle prayer, and as each of the two, three or four points of the address is made, a Celtic prayer is added as a meditative punctuation mark, that again can help to give a pause and remind everyone that this is a meditation for the soul, not just a lecture. The prayers in the sections on *Home* or *Work* are obvious examples where such a connection is useful when used in conjunction with material from the *Meditations* section.

There is no reason why any of these prayers should not be adapted for group or responsive use, and ideally they will spark the imagination for creating personal prayers too. As with all such prayers, they are best when said gently and slowly, giving people time to reflect and take in the subtleties of the imagery.

enjoying god's world 1

Delightful it is to stand on the peak of a rock,
in the bosom of the isle, gazing on the face of the sea.

I hear the heaving waves chanting a tune to God in heaven;
I see their glittering surf.

I see the gold beaches, their sands sparkling;
I hear the joyous shrieks of the swooping gulls.

I hear the waves breaking, crashing on rocks, like thunder in
heaven.
I see the mighty whales.

I watch the ebb and flow of the ocean tide:
it holds my secret, my mournful flight from Eire.

Contrition fills my heart as I hear the sea;
it chants my sins, sins too numerous to confess.

Let me bless almighty God, whose power extends over sea
and land, whose angels watch over all.

Let me study sacred books to calm my soul;
I pray for peace, kneeling at heaven's gates.

Let me do my daily work, gathering seaweed,
catching fish, giving food to the poor.

Let me say my daily prayers, sometimes chanting, sometimes
quiet,
always thanking God.

Delightful it is to live on a peaceful isle, in a quiet cell,
serving the King of kings.

Attributed to Columba, from *Celtic Fire* by Robert Van de Weyer

I wish, ancient and eternal King,
to live in a hidden hut in the wilderness.

A narrow blue stream beside it,
and a clear pool for washing away my sins
by the grace of the Holy Spirit.

A beautiful wood all around,
where birds of every kind of voice can grow up and find shelter.

Facing southwards to catch the sun,
with fertile soil around it suitable for every kind of plant.

And virtuous young men to join me,
humble and eager to serve God.

Twelve young men – three fours, four threes, two sixes, six
pairs –
willing to do every kind of work

A lovely church,
with a white linen cloth over the altar,
a home for God from heaven.

A Bible surrounded by four candles,
one for each of the gospels.

A special hut in which to gather for meals,
talking cheerfully as we eat,
without sarcasm, without boasting,
without any evil words.

Hens laying eggs for us to eat,
leeks growing near the stream,
salmon and trout to catch,
and bees providing honey.

Enough food and clothing
given by our Heavenly King,
and enough time to sit and pray to him.

Traditional (source unknown) from *Celtic Fire* by Robert Van de Weyer

enjoying god's world 2

I am the wind that breathes upon the sea,
I am the wave on the ocean,
I am the murmur of leaves rustling,
I am the rays of the sun,
I am the beam of the moon and stars,
I am the power of trees growing,
I am the bud breaking into blossom,
I am the movement of the salmon swimming,
I am the courage of the wild boar fighting,
I am the speed of the stag running,
I am the strength of the ox pulling the plough,
I am the size of the mighty oak tree,
And I am the thoughts of all people
Who praise my beauty and grace.

From 'The Black Book of Camarthen',
in *Celtic Fire* by Robert Van de Weyer

I would like to have the men of heaven
In my own house:
With vats of good cheer
Laid out for them.

I would like to have all the saints,
Their fame is so great.
I would like people
From every corner of heaven.

I would like them to be cheerful
In their drinking.
I would like to have Jesus too
Here amongst them.

I would like a great lake of beer
For the King of Kings,
I would like to be watching heaven's family
Drinking it through all eternity.

Source unknown (tenth century)

58

I have had enough
of sad saints
and sour religion.

I have had enough
of sin spotting
and grace doubting.
I need some laughter, Lord,
the kind you planted in Sarah.

But, please may I not have to wait
until I am ninety
and pregnant.

Church of Scotland

on pilgrimage
with god 1

Come I this day to the Father,
Come I this day to the Son,
Come I to the Holy Spirit powerful;
Come I this day with God,
Come I this day with Christ,
Come I with the Spirit of kindly balm.

God, and Spirit, and Jesus,
From the crown of my head
To the soles of my feet;
Come I with my reputation,
Come I with my testimony,
Come I to Thee, Jesu –
Jesu, shelter me.

Carmina Gadelica

God be with thee in every pass,
Jesus be with thee on every hill,
Spirit be with thee on every stream,
Headland and ridge and lawn;

Each sea and land, each moor and meadow,
Each lying down, each rising up,
In the trough of the waves, on the crest of the billows,
Each step of the journey thou goest.

Carmina Gadelica

My walk this day with God,
My walk this day with Christ,
My walk this day with Spirit,
The Threefold all-kindly:
Ho! ho! ho! the Threefold all-kindly.

My shielding this day from ill,
My shielding this night from harm,
Ho! Ho! both my soul and my body,
Be by Father, by Son, by Holy Spirit:
By Father, by Son, by Holy Spirit.

Be the Father shielding me,
Be the Son shielding me,
Be the Spirit shielding me,
As Three and as One.

Carmina Gadelica

May the strength of God pilot us.
May the power of God preserve us.
May the wisdom of God instruct us.
May the hand of God protect us.
May the way of God direct us.
May the shield of God defend us.
May the host of God guard us
Against the snares of the evil one
And the temptations of the world.
May Christ be with us
Christ above us
Christ in us
Christ before us.
May thy salvation O Lord,
Be always ours
This day and for evermore.
Amen.

St Patrick (fifth century)

on pilgrimage with god 2

Shall I leave the soft comforts of home, O Lord,
and be without money, power, and honour?
Shall I launch my little boat on the great sparkling ocean,
and go on my own on the deep?
Shall I leave the prints of my knees
on my own native land
and face the lonely sea?
Stand by me, God,
when it comes to the wild waves.

St Brendan

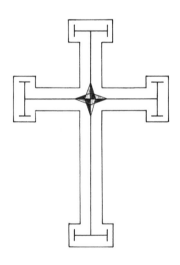

Bless to me, O God,
The earth beneath my foot,
Bless to me, O God,
The path whereon I go;
Bless to me, O God,
The thing of my desire;
Thou Evermore of evermore,
Bless thou to me my rest.

Bless to me the thing
Whereon is set my mind,
Bless to me the thing
Whereon is set my love;
Bless to me the thing
Whereon is set my hope;
O thou King of kings,
Bless thou to me mine eye!

Carmina Gadelica

I make my circuit
in the fellowship of my God
on the machair,* in the meadow,
on the cold heathery hill,
on the corner in the open,
on the chill windy dock,
to the noise of drills blasting,
to the sound of children asking.
I make my circuit
in the fellowship of my God
in city street
or on spring-turfed hill,
in shop-floor room
or at office desk.

God has no favourite places.
There are no special things.
All are God's and all is sacred.

I tread each day
in light or dark
in the fellowship of my God.

Be the sacred Three of glory
interwoven with our lives
until the Man who walks with us
leads us home
through death to life.

*machair – long coastal sandy plains
covered in flowers and grass

Kate McIlhagga (based on a prayer
from *Carmina Gadelica*), from *The Pattern of our Days*

As you were in the ebb and flow,
as the beginning becomes the ending,
and the ending a new beginning,
be with us
ever present God.

Kate McIlhagga (based on a prayer
from *Carmina Gadelica*), from *The Pattern of our Days*

in the home 1

Be Christ's cross on your new dwelling,
Be Christ's cross on your new hearth,
Be Christ's cross on your new abode,
Upon your new fire blazing.

Be Christ's cross on your topmost grain,
Be Christ's cross on your fruitful wives,
Be Christ's cross on your virile sons,
Upon your conceiving daughters.

Be Christ's cross on your means and portion,
Be Christ's cross on your kin and people,
Be Christ's cross on you each light and darkness,
Each day and each night of your lives,
Each day and each night of your lives.

Carmina Gadelica

God give grace
To this dwelling place

Christ give grace
To this dwelling place

Spirit give grace
To this dwelling place

David Adam

I smoor* the fire this night
As the Son of Mary would smoor it;
The compassing of God be on the fire,
The compassing of God on all the household.

Be God's compassing about ourselves,
Be God's compassing about us all,
Be God's compassing upon the flock,
Be God's compassing upon the hearth.

Who keeps watch this night?
Who but the Christ of the poor,
The bright and gentle Brigit of the kine,

The bright and gentle Mary of the ringlets.
Whole be house and herd,
Whole be son and daughter,
Whole be wife and man,
Whole be household all.

*smoor – smother with peat so that the fire smoulders until morning

Bless to us, O God
the doors we open
the thresholds we cross
the roads that lie before us.
Go with us as we go
and welcome us home.

Kate McIlhagga, from *The Pattern of our Days*

Peace be in my life
Peace be to my wife
Peace be to my children small
Peace be on all who call
Peace of the Father be mine
Peace of the Saviour entwine
Peace of the Spirit enthral
Peace of the Three be on all

David Adam

The Father is in the house
Nothing need we fear

Christ is in the house
Loving us so dear

The Spirit is in the house
Listening to our prayer

The Three are in the house
Always very near

David Adam

They will not throw you out
whilst your fire burns.
They have not that power.
Therefore keep your fire burning.

(In Scotland in earlier times householders could
not be evicted whilst the hearth fire was alight)

James Ayton

in the home 2

The peace of God, the peace of men,
The peace of Columba kindly,
The peace of Mary mild, the loving,
The peace of Christ, King of tenderness,
The peace of Christ, King of tenderness.

Be upon each window, upon each door,
Upon each hole that lets in light,
Upon the four corners of my house,
Upon the four corners of my bed,
Upon the four corners of my bed.

Upon each thing my eye takes in,
Upon each thing my mouth takes in,
Upon my body that is of earth
And upon my soul that came from on high.
Upon my body that is of earth
And upon my soul that came from on high.

Carmina Gadelica

God bless this house from roof to floor
God bless the windows and the door
God bless us all evermore
God bless the house with warmth and light
God bless each room with thy might
God with thy hand keep us right
God be with us in this dwelling site.

David Adam

O God, bless my homestead,
Bless Thou all therein.

O God, bless my kindred,
Bless Thou my substance.

O God, bless my words,
Bless Thou my converse.

O God, bless my errand,
Bless Thou my journey.

O God, lessen my sin,
Increase Thou my trust.

O God, ward from me distress.
Ward Thou from me misfortune.

O God, shield me from guilt,
Fill Thou me with joy.

And, O God, let naught to my body
That shall do harm to my soul

When I enter the fellowship
Of the great Son of Mary.

Carmina Gadelica

You called me in.
You sat me down.
You took my coat.
A cup you found.

You poured a drink.
You lent an ear.
You found a rag
For my tear.

You took a loaf
And with a knife,
You cut a piece
To revive my life.

You held the door.
Your hand you waved.
You gave your smile
For another soul saved.

James Ayton

Bless the father of this house
Bless the father and his spouse
Bless the children growing tall
Bless the family one and all

Peace be upon all within
Peace to keep you free from sin
Peace upon your neighbours all
Peace be upon those who call

David Adam

at mealtimes

Warmth to our stomachs
Warmth to our souls
In the warmth
Of the God of Peace

God in our mouths
and in our digesting
God in our mouths
and in our conversation

Good food and the strength of God
Good food and the love of Christ
Good food and the Spirit's presence
Be with us at this meal

John Davies

Bless, O Lord,
this food we are about to eat,
and we pray you, O God
that it may be good
for our body and soul,
and if there is any poor creature
hungry or thirsty walking the road
may God send him in to us
so that we can share the food with him,
just as Christ shares his gifts
with all of us.

From Shabbat, Blessings over food,
Celtic Night Prayer

Be with me, O God, at the breaking of bread,
Be with me, O God, at the end of my meal;
May no morsel of my body's partaking
Add to my soul's freight.

Thanks to you, O God,
Praise to you, O God,
Honour to you, O God,
For all you have given me.

You have given me bodily existence
To win me earthly food,
Grant me also immortal life
To reveal your glory.

Carmina Gadelica

O King of stars!
Whether my house be dark or bright,
Never shall it be closed against any one,
Lest Christ close His house against me.

If there be a guest in your house
And you conceal aught from him.
'Tis not the guest that will be without it,
But Jesus, Mary's Son.

Carmina Gadelica

I saw a stranger yester-even,
I put food in the eating place,
drink in the drinking place,
music in the listening place,
and in the sacred name of the Triune,
He blessed myself and my house,
my cattle and my dear ones,
and the lark said in her song
often, often, often
goes the Christ in the stranger's guise.

From *The Book of Cerne*

night and day 1

Dark is the night,
high is the mountain.
Cold is the stream,
high is the fountain.

Warm is the sun,
cool is the sea.
Strong are the waves
strength you give me.

Joanne Stephens

May the Light of lights come
To my dark heart from Thy place;
May the Spirit's wisdom come
To my heart's tablet from my Saviour.

Be the peace of the Spirit mine this night,
Be the peace of the Son mine this night,
Be the peace of the Father mine this night,
The peace of all peace be mine this night,
Each morning and evening of my life.

Carmina Gadelica

Be thou a bright flame before me,
be thou a guiding star above me,
be thou a smooth path below me,
be thou a kindly shepherd behind me
today, tonight, and for ever.

St Columba

There on the misted hills
I see a purple haze
My heart with joy infills
Father accept my praise.

There in the darkening skies
I see the brilliant stars
Christ of a thousand sighs
Your love my heart restores.

Here in the blush of dawn
I see God's Spirit rise
Salvation thus was born
And never ever dies.

Ramon Beeching

I lie down this night with God,
And God will lie down with me;
I lie down this night with Christ,
And Christ will lie down with me;
I lie down this night with Spirit,
And the Spirit will lie down with me;
God and Christ and the Spirit
Be lying down with me.

Carmina Gadelica

níght and day 2

Monday we see your creation
Tuesday we need your correction
Wednesday we seek your guidance
Thursday is full of silence
Friday we acknowledge your existence
Saturday you seem so distant
Sunday we unite with you in your church
On our journey for you in our search.

Joanne Stephens

May I speak this day according to Thy justice,
Each day may I show Thy chastening, O God;
May I speak each day according to Thy wisdom,
Each day and night may I be at peace with Thee.

Each day may I count the causes of Thy mercy,
May I each day give heed to Thy laws;
Each day may I compose to Thee a song,
May I harp each day Thy praise, O God.

May I each day give love to Thee, Jesu,
Each night may I do the same;
Each day and night, dark and light,
May I laud Thy goodness to me, O God.

Carmina Gadelica

On the holy Sunday of thy God
Give thou thine heart to all mankind,
To thy father and thy mother loving,
Beyond any person or thing in the world.

Do not covet large or small,
Do not despise weakling or poor,
Semblance of evil allow not near thee,
Never give nor earn thou shame.

The ten commands God gave thee,
Understand them early and prove,
Believe direct in the King of the elements,
Put behind thee ikon-worship.

Be faithful to thine over-lord,
Be true to thy King in every need,
Be true to thine own self besides,
True to thy High-King above all obstacles.

Do not malign any man,
Less thou thyself maligned shouldst be,
And shouldst thou travel ocean and earth,
Follow the very steps of God's Anointed.

Carmina Gadelica

O God, who broughtst me from the rest of last night
Unto the joyous light of this day,
Be Thou bringing me from the new light of this day
Unto the guiding light of eternity.
Oh! from the new light of this day
Unto the guiding light of eternity.

Carmina Gadelica

The eye of the great God,
The eye of the God of glory,
The eye of the King of hosts,
The eye of the King of the living,
Pouring upon us
At each time and season,
Pouring upon us
Gently and generously.

Glory to thee,
Thou glorious sun.

Glory to thee, thou sun,
Face of the God of life.

Carmina Gadelica

at work 1

I give my hands to you Lord
I give my hands to you

I offer the work I do Lord
I offer the work I do

I give my thoughts to you Lord
I give my thoughts to you

I give my plans to you Lord
I give my plans to you

Give your hands to me Lord
Give your hands to me

Let your love set me free Lord
Let your love set me free

Keep me close to you Lord
Keep me close to you.

David Adam

Be thou my battle-shield, be thou my sword:
be thou my honour, be thou my delight.

Be thou my shelter, be thou my stronghold:
mayest thou raise me up in the company of angels.

Be thou every good to my body and soul:
be thou my kingdom in heaven and earth.

Be thou alone my heart's special love:
let there be none other save the High-king of heaven.

To the King of all may I come after prized practice of devotion:
may I be in the kingdom of heaven in the brightness of the sun.

Beloved Father, hear my lamentation:
this miserable wretch (alas!) thinks it time.

Beloved Christ, whate'er befalls me:
O Ruler of all, be thou my vision.

Eighth century Irish, source unknown

This morning, as I kindle the fire upon my hearth,
I pray that the flame of God's love may burn in my heart,
and the hearts of all I meet today.

I pray that no envy and malice, no hatred or fear,
may smother the flame.

I pray that indifference and apathy, contempt and pride,
may not pour like cold water on the fire.

Instead, may the spark of God's love light the love in my
heart, that it may burn brightly through the day.

And may I warm those that are lonely, whose hearts are cold
and lifeless, so that all may know the comfort of God's love.

Traditional, source unknown

Be Thou with us, O Chief of chiefs,
Be Thou Thyself to us
a compass-chart,
Be Thine hand on the helm of our rudder,
Thine own hand,
Thou God of the elements,
Early and late as is becoming,
Early and late as is becoming.

Bless our boatmen and our boat,
Bless our anchors and our oars,
Each stay and halyard and traveller.

Carmina Gadelica

I create this report in the name of Father.
I save this report in the name of the Son.
I edit this report in the name of the Spirit.

Beth Rogers

at work 2

Grant us a vision, Lord,
To see what we can achieve
To reach out beyond ourselves
To share our lives with others
To stretch our capabilities
To increase our sense of purpose
To be aware of where we can help
To be sensitive to your Presence
To give heed to your constant call.

David Adam

Remember the poor when you look out on fields you own,
on your plump cows grazing.

Remember the poor when you look into your barn,
at the abundance of your harvest.

Remember the poor when the wind howls and the rain falls,
as you sit warm and dry in your house.

Remember the poor when you eat fine meat and drink fine
ale at your fine carved table.

The cows have grass to eat, the rabbits have burrows for
shelter, the birds have warm nests.

But the poor have no food except what you feed them,
no shelter except your house when you welcome them,
no warmth except your glowing fire.

Traditional, from *Celtic Fire* by Robert Van de Weyer

Lord,
Reveal in us your glory
Stir in us your power
Open in us your love
Work in us your miracles
Show in us your way
Renew in us your kingdom
Abide in us Yourself.

David Adam

Lord,
Whatever we build,
Give us a glimpse of glory.
Whatever we make,
Give us a sense of wonder.
Wherever we travel,
Give us a sense of reverence.
Whoever we meet,
Give us a sense of awe.
Whatever we do,
Give us a sense of achievement.
Whatever our situation,
Give us knowledge of you.

David Adam

Call, Call, Call, great Chief of the high hills;
Call, Call, Call, great Christ of the far paths;
Call, Call, Call, great Counsellor of the near gate.

Set my spirit free to soar where'er you climb;
Set my feet free to trek where'er you go;
Set my hands free to do what'er you say.

A response:
I resolve to find and follow my vocation.

Ray Simpson

how to compose a celtic blessing

Praying cannot just be about lifting words from a page and reciting them. It is about opening our hearts and minds to the living spirit of God. Similarly, creating new prayers is not just about composing literary masterpieces. It is about using the gifts God has given to lift ourselves beyond the mundane. The ancient Celtic Christians had discovered such ways of encountering our extraordinary God in the ordinary events of daily life. When Alexander Carmichael made his Hebridean collection of Celtic poems and prayers in the nineteenth century (the *Carmina Gadelica*) he included prayers about milking cows, making cheese, digging peat, washing clothes, and weaving cloth. In other words, he recorded a spirituality of the normal day, not one that belonged only in the church service.

Personal experience shows that to pray about these things but in a trinitarian and a very simple poetic way can be both enjoyable and uplifting. It can be done while waiting in the supermarket queue and become a gentle prayer for those shopping or working behind the checkout. It can transform the traffic hold-up from an irritating nuisance to an opportunity for creative prayer about those in surrounding cars. Moreover, the more it is done the easier and more natural it becomes.

Below are just some examples of what has been produced in workshops, often by those who began by protesting they could not do it!

Take *any* normal action of the day: waking up, washing, writing, digging, eating, etc.

A   Now **think Trinity**: e.g. driving the car:
I drive my car in the name of the Father,
I drive my car in the name of the Son,
I drive my car in the name of the Spirit.

B   Next, **analyse the action**: i.e. divide the action chosen into three component parts:
I steer my car in the name of the Father,
I drive my car carefully in the name of the Son,
I navigate my car in the name of the Spirit.

C   Then, ask God to be active in what you do and make it theologically trinitarian:
make the first line about the Father and his creating;
the second line about the Son and his salvation or redeeming power;
the third line about the Spirit and his help or enabling.
And also make it into a simple **rhyme**:

> *Father, give wisdom as I steer,*
> *Son, save us from all fear,*
> *Spirit, guide till at home we appear.*

One needs to allow forty-five minutes at first, taking it slowly stage by stage to be sure every-one is ready to move on to the next step. Do not worry about how infantile it seems. When this is attempted in groups as part of a workshop, it is usually the case that as people share their prayers with each other, there is no great ridicule but rather very affirmative remarks indeed.

So, making the bed can be transformed from a chore to a reminder of God's involvement in life:

> *I make this bed in the name of the Father,*
> *I make this bed in the name of the Son,*
> *I make this bed in the name of the Spirit,*
> *I make this bed in the name of the night I was conceived,*
> *I make this bed in the name of the night I was born,*
> *I make this bed in the name of the night I was baptised.*

This can be developed further as these two examples show:

> *God who made us, we worship you.*
> *Christ who saved us, we thank you.*
> *Spirit who strengthens us, we need you.*
> > *God the Father bless our days.*
> > *God the Son we give you praise.*
> > *God the Spirit guide our ways*
> > *Now and evermore. Amen.*

> *God the creator, renew this plant's growth.*
> *Christ the carpenter, bless the use of this tool.*
> *Spirit who guides, control my hand's work.*
> *Father of life, bless your good earth.*
> *Son who redeems, give gardens new birth.*
> *Spirit enlightening, show us their worth.*

> both by Daphne Bridges, from *Pocket Celtic Prayers*

Beth Rogers, with a sense of humour and an eye for trinitarian theology, composed a prayer about her use of the computer at work:

> *I create this report in the name of the Father,*
> *I save[!] this report in the name of the Son,*
> *I edit this report in the name of the Spirit. Amen.*

Marvellous! This can be attempted alone or as a group: the results are fun, very revealing, and often display hidden talent!

lessons from the saints

ɪɴᴛʀᴏᴅᴜᴄᴛɪᴏɴ

What stories will be told about us when we are long gone? The fourth to ninth centuries in this country are known as the Dark Ages because we apparently know so little and Europe was in decline following the collapse of the Roman Empire.

However, there were spiritual giants in the land! These were people who pioneered a disciplined and communal approach to living and sharing the Christian faith, and many of them have their lives recorded as hagiographies – stories about saints that are meant to inspire later readers. Clearly some of these stories seem quite plausible, some have a ring of truth about them, and some are patently absurd, all depending on our own preconceived notion of miracles.

What is astounding, however, is that most of the stories grew up around these saints very quickly after their death. There would still be alive those who knew these people personally and who could contradict the stories if they were not in keeping with the saints' characters. That means that these stories must have contained at least a core of truth and must have been in keeping with the achievements of the saint.

In other words, while they may not all quite literally be 'true stories' they are certainly meant to be 'stories with a truth' Approached in that way, these tales take on a quite fresh and liberating feel. As these stories are read and expanded dramatically in the retelling (for they are written here in a very stark way through limitations of space), so we are meant to be led to ask, '*what lessons do these have for my life today?*' And perhaps even more important, '*what stories will people be telling about me in years to come?*'

The accounts recorded here are obviously written in a very simple and compact way. While it might be possible just to read them to a group of people, it is obviously much better if the story-teller makes them her or his own, adding emotion and just a little colour to the accounts. They were never written originally just to be factual, but rather to engage the heart as well as the mind and lead people on to consider their own lives. The telling as much as the content is what encourages inspiration.

st ninian of whithorn

When Ninian was born around AD 360 his father, a Celtic chieftain in Cumbria, was battling against Picts, Gaels and Angles eager to take control in the vacuum left by the departure of the Romans. He was keen his son should become a warrior, but had not reckoned on Ninian's later desire to become a warrior for Christ. When he was eighteen years old Ninian decided he wanted deeper instruction about the Christian faith, and so he left for Rome. At the end of his time there the Pope consecrated him a missionary bishop. On his way home in AD 387 he stayed with St Martin of Tours in his embryonic monastery.

That experience with Martin so impressed him that when he returned to Whithorn he set about establishing the first Celtic monastery in Britain, where it became known as 'Candida Casa' – glistening white house. The same word is used to describe the glistening white that encompassed Jesus at the time of his transfiguration when Moses and Elijah appeared with him. In 1952 archaeologists discovered walls three feet thick, covered in white mortar, but the name was as much to do with the light of Christ as with its physical appearance, and many legends abound of this bearer of the light of Christ.

Ninian shone a spotlight on truth

One story involves a servant girl who became pregnant by her master. Not unnaturally she was afraid to reveal the identity of the true father, and so publicly accused the local priest. Ninian heard about this and called the baptised people together in order to discover the truth. As he baptized the child, Ninian commanded the baby to indicate his true father. With a gurgling noise the baby pointed at the father and the painful truth was faced. Unlike so many today, Ninian was not one with an appetite for scandal but for truth. Like Jesus, he was unafraid to expose the truth, show moral nerve, and confront scandal.

Ninian upheld a torch of purity

Ninian's prayers were never trivial. One day, resting with a companion by the road, Ninian began reading his Bible. Even as it rained the drops did not fall on the pages because of the purity of Ninian's mind. However, secret lustful thoughts crept into his heart and his scriptures began to spoil as the rains dampened the ink. His companion noticed and Ninian blushed with embarrassment and repented immediately. In an age when moral purity is not always held high even among Christians, Ninian's example upholds Jesus' teaching that sins of the mind are as real as sins of the flesh.

Ninian lit a flame of holistic healing

On another occasion, the local king, Tuduvallus, who opposed Ninian's work, had become blind. As the king he realized the power of this new Christian faith and knew it to be a force to be reckoned with. But in his despair he asked Ninian to pray for him. Ninian first scolded him for his previous lack of faith, made the sign of the cross on his eyelids and the king repented. As he opened his eyes so he found his sight had been restored. Ninian showed he understood, as did Jesus, the relationship between the state of the soul and the state of the body: spiritual and physical sight were treated together. As Jesus healed the blind man and then immediately went on to describe himself as the Light of the World, so Ninian was being true to that holistic approach.

Ninian fanned a beacon of spiritual power

One night as he spent the night with some shepherds, he prayed a protecting 'caim' circle-prayer around them before going to sleep. Under cover of darkness thieves tried to steal some sheep, but as they crossed the invisible circle a bull rushed and gored one of the robbers. Ninian awoke, realized what had happened, and healed the thief. As they knelt in awe asking for forgiveness, Ninian pronounced his pardon on them all, and allowed them to leave.

Here was someone who not only believed but practised the power of prayer to protect, heal, pardon and release. As he lay dying at the age of 71 he heard a voice saying:

> Arise and hasten,
> My friend,
> My dove,
> And come,
> Arise my friend,
> Arise my dove,
> Arise through the mind.
> Hasten by desire,
> Hasten by love.

Here was a man who knew the reality of God, the reality of faith, the reality of spiritual power, and the reality of heaven.

The flame of Christianity was kept bright with Ninian. He shone in the so-called Dark Ages following Jesus' command: 'Let your light so shine before people, that they may see your good works and glorify your Father in heaven.'

Group reflections

1. If Jesus is the Light of the World, in what ways has he illuminated your life? Be specific with examples.

2. In the Sermon on the Mount, Jesus told his disciples that they were to be light in the world. List three ways in which you have tried to shine as the light of Christ in the last month.

3. Tackling the truth about a situation, especially in Christian circles, can be risky and painful. Can you give an example where this has been avoided recently? Was there an alternative way?

4. In what ways could your church become increasingly, like Ninian's monastery, a *Candida Casa*, a community sparkling with Christ's love? Choose just one focus for attention and create a plan of action.

st patrick of ireland

'Magonus Sucatos Patricius' hardly sounds a very Irish name! That is because St Patrick was not Irish but was born in Cumbria about AD 390 from a wealthy family in which his father had been a deacon and his grandfather a priest. But in his early years his faith was only nominal and his reputation was wild. At sixteen he was captured by pirates and sold as a slave in Armagh where he was forced into work as a shepherd. There he met committed Christians and his faith developed and became real. By the age of 23 he was a thoroughly converted believer. 'I used to pray a hundred prayers by day and a further hundred by night, through snow, frost and rain' he later wrote, 'I had no inclination to take things easy because the Spirit *seethed* in me.'

Visions and voices

Six years on, one night he dreamt of a boat waiting for him. He escaped, walked 200 miles, found the boat of his vision and sailed for Gaul. One tradition tells us that he spent time with his uncle, Martin of Tours, before returning to his home. Once home, however, he heard a voice calling him to return to Ireland as a missionary: 'Come back and walk with us once more.' At first he was refused permission because of his past wild reputation, but eventually he was consecrated a missionary bishop and allowed to return to the country of his captors. He was returning to a place where new Christians were butchered and Christian women were deliberately sold in the market as prostitute slaves. Once in Ireland there were many attempts on his life and he was engaged in many conflicts, the most important of which recalls the battle between Elijah and the prophets of Baal on Mount Carmel.

Hills and fires

The greatest Druidic fire-festival culminated at the spring equinox, and focused on the Hill of Tara where the High Kings were crowned. All other fires were banned, so that the full drama was realized. Patrick decided the time had come for the light of Christ to replace the pagan fires. As it was also Easter-eve, he lit his own paschal fire on the nearby Hill of Slane. The king's advisers knew that if Patrick's fire was not extinguished this new faith would flood Ireland. Soldiers were sent but Patrick escaped – the fire had been lit, and Ireland was to become a Christian stronghold. Within thirty years he had built 360 churches, ordained hundreds of clergy, and even he was embarrassed at his success.

He worked tirelessly, with only one story of a break when he spent forty days fasting and praying on the hill now known as Croagh Patrick. On that hill on the last Saturday in July thousands still walk to the top, often barefoot, in memory of Patrick.

Two writings

His two attributed writings, the *Confessions* and the *Breastplate* are consistent with a man who knew the love of God which inspires complete devotion, and the reality of spiritual warfare which demands serious attention to putting on the armour of God. He understood that grace is never cheap nor Christian living casual. His was no mere 'Sunday religion'. On one occasion when he was asked by the daughters of the King of Connaught, 'Who is your King?' he replied:

> Our king is the king of all,
> Heaven and earth,
> Sea and river:
> He has his dwelling
> In Heaven and earth and sea,
> And all that is therein.
> He inspires all things,
> He quickens all things.
> He kindles the light
> Of the sun and the moon.
> He has a Son co-eternal with himself
> And like unto him.
> And the Holy Spirit breathes in them.
> Father, Son, and Holy Spirit are not divided.
> And I desire to unite you
> To the Son of the Heavenly king
> For you are daughters of a king of earth.

Such a creed, adapted for the particular missionary occasion, has much to commend itself.

The *Breastplate* is the oldest Irish document in existence, and although it is attributed to the ninth century, its language is clearly archaic and belongs to a previous time. Throughout, its focus is clearly Jesus, and Patrick draws on New Testament imagery of the armour of God, the communion of saints as portrayed in the Epistle to the Hebrews, and is thoroughly trinitarian throughout.

As Patrick's great influence is recalled, so we are called to pray for Patrick's Ireland today. Reconciliation between person and person, and reconciliation between person and God was what he was all about . . . and what we are surely also about.

Group reflections

1. Patrick's direct experiences of God are similar to those of Noah, Abraham, Moses, and the prophets of the Old Testament. In the New Testament Paul saw visions and heard voices. Do you honestly think God still puts pictures and words in our minds?

2. How would you describe your direct experiences of the presence and call of God?

3.   How has your individual experience of God fired your desire to share the Christian gospel effectively?

4.   Give one example of how your evangelism has been confrontational and one of how it has been more enfolding and welcoming. Which has been more effective and why?

st BRÍGÍd of kÍLDaRe

For everything that Brigid asked of the Lord was granted her at once. For this was her desire: to satisfy the poor, to expel every hardship, to spare every miserable man. Now there never has been anyone more demure, or more modest, or more gentle, or more humble, or wiser, or more harmonious than Brigid. She never washed her hands, or head, or feet among men. She never looked at the face of a man. She would never speak without blushing. She was abstinent. She was innocent. She was prayerful. She was patient. She was glad in God's commandments. She was firm. She was humble. She was forgiving. She was loving. She was a consecrated casket for Christ. She was a temple of God. Her heart and her mind were a throne of rest for the Holy Spirit. She was simple towards God. She was compassionate towards the wretched. She was splendid in miracles and marvels.

(The Book of Lismore)

What an epitaph!

Brigid was undoubtedly the most famous of all the female Celtic Christians. She was a contemporary of Patrick, born around the year AD 452, and her whole life seems to be concerned with managing and crossing boundaries.

Paganism and Christianity

She was even born on the boundary between paganism and Christianity. Her mother was a slave girl who had been made pregnant by her master. The master's wife found out, and ordered her husband to sell the girl. Eventually she was sold on through several other people to a Druid, and it was *as she crossed the threshold of his door* that she gave birth to Brigid. The story is symbolic of Brigid's life. At that time Ireland was still pagan. It was on the threshold of becoming Christian.

Material and spiritual wealth

Brigid was somebody who stood on the boundary between material and spiritual wealth. As she grew, everything she touched seemed to go well but she was incredibly generous with her father's possessions and kept giving away everything he had to those who called at the door! The last straw came for her father when she gave away his favourite sword to a leper. In exasperation, he took her to the king. The king questioned Brigid, but her answer to him was simple: 'Jesus knows, if I had your wealth, my Lord, I would give it all to God!' The king's reply was equally simple: 'Her God is higher than ours!'

Sexism and inequality

Brigid also stood on the boundary between sexism and equality. Her father tried to arrange a marriage for her when she was eighteen. She refused to comply, but did respond to a vocation to be a nun. Because of her humility, she stood at the end of the row waiting to be accepted into the order, and while she waited the bishop saw a fiery pillar above her head raised to the roof. He said, 'Come, holy Brigid, that a veil may be placed over your head before all the others.' Then, by mistake it is said, he read from the wrong service, and made her a bishop! Other priests present objected because she was a woman, but the bishop responded, 'I have no power. That dignity has already been given her by God!'

During her lifetime she founded many churches, but the most famous was the convent she established at Kildare, in the central plain of Ireland. It became known as 'the City of the Poor' because of her hospitality. There she lit a fire and the task of maintaining it was given to twenty nuns, including herself, whose job it was to keep that fire alight as a symbol of faith. After she had died, nineteen nuns traditionally kept the flame alive, and it was, in fact, kept alight for a thousand years after her time, until the dissolution of the monasteries.

Chill winds of life and the warmth of God's love

Brigid was also somebody who crossed the boundary between the chill winds of life and the warmth of God's love. The story is told of the time when she was staying at a convent just before Easter. It was the tradition on Maundy Thursday for the abbess to ask for a volunteer to care for the old, the weak and the feeble. When called, none of the nuns volunteered, and so Brigid put herself forward. While she was doing her duty, four people came to call at the door: a leper, a blind person, a deranged man, and one with consumption. All were healed, but it did not surprise the others as Brigid had a powerful reputation for a ministry of healing.

There were many stories of her powers over nature. For example, stone was turned to salt when needed, water to milk, food was increased to feed a crowd like that at the feeding of the 5,000 and water was turned to beer. Stories abound too of her evangelistic activities. There is a particular story that on one occasion she was tending a dying pagan king. As she sat beside him, she absent-mindedly plaited a cross from some straw. When the king asked what she was doing, she explained what the cross was all about, and before he died he became a Christian.

Brigid's cross

Instructions for making a St Brigid's cross can be found in this book (p.167). On St Brigid's Day, 1 February, in some places in Ireland the cross is still hung up in the house. The next year on the same date, a new cross is hung in the house and the old one is hung in the stable. The following year, another new cross is hung in the house, the previous one now hung in the stable, and the original one is ploughed into the fields. It is a symbolic way of praying for blessing on the house, the animals, and the crops.

Group reflections

Jesus is the 'great high priest' (Hebrews 4.14) who has crossed the boundary between heaven and earth, time and eternity. We are called to be a 'royal priesthood' (1 Peter 2.9) helping others cross spiritual boundaries. Brigid certainly did that.

1. Identify three major boundaries that exist in your community (perhaps fear, loneliness, materialism or busyness) that prevent people enjoying the love of God.

2. Share how you have crossed those boundaries yourselves.

3. How might you help others both identify and cross these boundaries into a full and rich relationship with God?

st Brendan
of the oceans

Born in AD 489 in Tralee, south-west Ireland, Brendan was brought up on stories of the biblical travellers – Noah, Abraham, Moses and even Jonah, the reluctant pilgrim! He learned about the mystical Island of Promise over the horizon, a place full of light, fragrant flowers, fruit, and where all the stones were jewels. Brendan consulted with his fellow monks and he fasted for 40 days during which time he saw a vision in which an angel assured him he would see this island. He built a boat covering the frame with ox-hides and set off with fourteen companions.

They encountered many islands and experienced hospitable hermits, a fish as large as an island (a whale), an island of sparkling crystal (an iceberg), a barren island with a mountain spitting fire (a volcano), and great swarms of glittering fish. His descriptions tell us he travelled by the Faroe Islands, Iceland, Greenland, and Newfoundland, and suggest he skirted back by the Azores and Spain. He returned home enriched but sad at not having found the Island of Promise after five years at sea, and settled into a ministry of healings, exorcism and teaching. His mother then explained (after the event!) that using the skins of killed animals would prevent him landing on an ideal island, for he would spoil its innocence!

Setting out again, this time in a wooden boat, he discovered the island where he was invited ashore and found it beyond his dreams. The island was a place of health, joy, feasting, meadows and angels. But to his great sadness, he was told to leave before he tainted it. Two years later he returned home, this time a fulfilled person.

What are we to learn from his journeys? How are we to interpret the stories?

1.   An allegory

We gain nothing by failing to venture out into the big wide ocean of life. Life is a voyage full of dangers with possible shipwrecks, monsters and enemies, as well as surprising generosity from unexpected strangers. Sometimes we can be tested by new adventures as we go with the currents and tides of life. Occasionally we discover new insights, wisdom, knowledge and faith, and at very special times we glimpse a vision of paradise itself. If we are spiritually alive at all, then we will find we are tested *and* blessed as we venture out from the safety of our harbours.

2.   A discovery

While Brendan and his monks sailed they kept strictly to all the monastic times of devotion, being a 'floating monastery'. Feasts, festivals, and fasts were all observed. The rules and structure they kept were the basis of their security, not the purpose of their existence. Disciplined in the prayer routine, they were ready to take on new insights and horizons and experiences. The faith of the sailors was a framework for the journey not a cage to imprison them. Today, so often, churches seem to contain many adults who have grown physically, mentally and emotionally, but not spiritually. Consequently, when faced with complex moral or ethical issues, the simple 'Sunday School' maxims are not seen to be applicable. Faith is then seen as having nothing to do with real life. Risking new styles of praying, worship, relating, or applying biblical stories to social issues is feared. Launching out into the unknown with God was clearly something Brendan longed to do, and consequently he grew as a person.

3. A focus

Brendan travelled *with* the Lord rather than setting out to find him. He knew Jesus as the 'pioneer', the 'way, the truth and the life' (John 14.6). Like the early disciples he understood Jesus as someone always on the move, and set out to go with his Spirit discovering more about him along the way. He understood that while the Island of Promise was a destination, in fact it was the journey itself that was the real destination. Even on his first journey, although he returned disappointed because he failed to find that elusive island, he did, in fact, return a different person with a very powerful ministry.

4. A reminder

Brendan died aged 90, and only then did he really set foot on the true Island of Promise. His death was simply another voyage to discover even more of Jesus in the great Island of Promise – heaven.

There is a story about a Himalayan explorer who, when very old, set out to climb a steep mountain. The weather was very bitter and cold. When asked, 'How do you know you will make it?' he replied, 'My heart is there already: so it is easy for the rest to follow.' That story is almost a parable about the life of Brendan, a Celtic Christian on a physical and spiritual pilgrimage.

Group reflections

1. The first disciples followed Jesus for a journey into the unknown. What today hinders us from being true to Jesus' call, 'Follow me'?

2. What *practical* difference has your Christian obedience made to your life?

3. How would you say your spiritual life has grown deeper over the past five years?

4. What uncharted waters has your church launched out into over the past year? What new things has God called you to explore?

5. What have these experiences taught you about God?

6. Social action, evangelism, worship, links with other groups, missionary support, spiritual development: where do you think God wants you to go this year?

st columba of íona

Ireland

A royal prince, Columba was born in Donegal in AD 521, his mother having had a vision of a cloak stretching out, foretelling that her son's teaching would stretch across both Ireland and Scotland. He was brought up as a Christian, and in his teens asked God for three virtues: chastity, wisdom, and pilgrimage. At nineteen he was accepted into a monastery and took the name 'Columcille', meaning 'Dove of the Church'. Today we refer to him simply as 'Columba'.

He established his first monastery at the age of 25 at Derry, now Londonderry, on an existing Druidic sacred site, and during his lifetime founded over 300 churches and monasteries.

Everything went well until he was in his forties. He copied a psalter from another monk's parchment and then claimed the copy was his. A great copyright argument broke out and a wise old man ruled that 'the calf belongs to the cow' – the copy belongs with the original. Columba's fiery temper broke and he called on his father's army. In a huge battle thousands were killed! Horrified at what he had caused to happen, Columba decided on self-imposed exile, not resting until he had converted at least as many as the number of deaths he had caused as a penance. So he left, not settling until he could no longer see his beloved homeland – and so his base was established on Iona.

Iona

From Iona (which coincidentally also means 'Dove') he travelled, converting both kings and commoners, and was such a workaholic that his monks often found him very trying. Iona itself was a good base: it was already a Druidic site and so had holy associations in people's minds; it was at the heart of the commercial seaways of the area; and it offered good opportunities for growing crops and grazing animals. He came to the island full of guilt and remorse but looking for resurrection. His faith was based on the story of Jesus: that faithfulness to God means Easter Sunday always follows Good Friday. He knew his God was one of action and there are many stories of him expelling spirits, calming wild animals, stilling storms and even saving a swimmer from the Loch Ness monster!

Columba was keen to convert the ordinary people, but he knew that first he had to win the rulers. Brude was King of the Picts at Inverness and Columba became political adviser to him early on. Clearly his strategy worked for at one time there were over a thousand monks on Iona. But he was not always easy to live with. After his death one monk wrote that 'he would not spend one hour without studying, praying and writing!' Workaholics can make difficult partners, but reconciliation was obviously high on his agenda.

One day he needed to cross some water. The oarsman of the boat was so ugly his wife would have nothing to do with him. 'I would rather *even be a man* than lie with him', she said. Columba suggested they all pray and fast for twenty-four hours, and at the end the wife said, 'yesterday I loathed that man but today I love him'. Naturally, as with all good stories, they all lived happily ever after.

He was also unafraid to speak God's word boldly. On one occasion a servant-boy wanted simply to touch the great man, but others considered the boy too lowly and tried to push him away (rather like the disciples who tried to keep the little children away from Jesus). But Columba, seeing him, touched the boy's mouth, prophesying that he would become a very great Christian leader, which is what happened. At another time, Columba was introduced to a very rich ruler, but was unimpressed by his wealth, this time prophesying that the man would die an impoverished wretch. Again, this is what happened.

Heaven

On Iona Columba even foretold his own death. He had asked God for 30 years on Iona but when the time drew near he asked for an extension of four years to complete his work. The time came, however, and one story records that even his horse shed tears as he lay dying. As Columba was carried around the island to bless it one final time, he prophesied that one day the island would return to being simply farmland, but that before the end of the world it would be returned as a place of mission – and that is exactly what has happened as the monastery was sacked in the ninth century by raiders and left desolate until the Iona Community was founded this century.

This man who was spied encircled by angels as he prayed, whose church was bathed in light as he prayed, whose cell shed light from its doorway as he prayed, demonstrates that from awful tragedies God can bring great blessing once repentance and true devotion are recognized as the keys to the future.

Group reflections

1. In Mark 1 Jesus' first words include a call to repent. Columba clearly acknowledged his mistake. Why is such language not fashionable today?

2. Can you give any examples of where you have laid before God a mistake and then seen an Easter Day dawn from your Good Friday?

3. God seems not only to like new people, but has fun giving people new names! Columba or Columcille means 'Dove of the Church'. Can you devise Christian nicknames for the members of your group just as Jesus renamed Simon, 'Peter' and Saul became 'Paul'?

4. Columba foresaw the future of the Island of Iona and how renewal would follow trouble. What do you foresee for your local community in, say, 100 years' time, and how might you build strong foundations for the church that will serve it?

st aidan of lindisfarne

King Oswald of Northumbria had been brought up in exile on Iona by Columba's monks. When he became king he asked for a missionary from Iona to convert his people, and a monk named Corman was sent. His mission, however, was a failure, and he described the people of the north-east as 'stupid, ignorant and stubborn'. At the meeting in Iona, Aidan suggested, 'it seems to me you were too severe on your ignorant hearers', and, as when anyone comes up with a good idea at a meeting, Aidan was the next to be sent to Northumbria!

Gentle

So in AD 635 Aidan and twelve companions set out for Northumbria, and chose the island of Lindisfarne as a base, only two miles from the king's castle at Bamburgh. Here he established his monastery. Whenever he set out on his missionary journeys, it was the king who accompanied him as his interpreter and his more gentle and loving approach was very successful.

At one Easter feast in the castle a great commotion outside was heard. It was reported that the people were starving. The king glanced at Aidan and then immediately ordered not only the food from the feast but also the silver crockery should be distributed to his hungry subjects. Aidan, overcome with emotion, grasped him saying, 'My Lord, may this hand never perish'. Years later when his coffin was opened, the king's hand was found to be well preserved! There are many other stories demonstrating Aidan's concern for the poor and the effect he had on those around him. Aidan's genuine concern for the poor and needy won him many converts.

Prayerful

One day Aidan saw rival king Penda attacking Bamburgh and attempting to set fire to the castle: he had pulled wood and straw from surrounding huts and used them as kindling. Aidan, without any frantic emotion, quietly knelt and prayed 'Lord, see what evil Penda does.' As he looked up he saw the wind turn towards the attackers, driving them away and leaving the castle safe. Many such miracles are attributed to Aidan, and Bede describes him as someone who was 'genuine, in whom God lived, whose life was not just words, who lived as he taught, who gave away all he had, who was prepared to criticise the powerful and care for the needy, who studied the gospels constantly: a man of peace, love, purity and humility.'

Local

When Aidan established his monastery on Lindisfarne one of the first things he did was to set up a school to train twelve local boys at a time as missionary-priests, teaching them literacy, the gospels and psalms, and spiritual disciplines. By training local Saxon youngsters he was able to work from within the local culture. Christianity thus could become a local rather than an imposed faith. His love of local people is revealed in the most famous story about him.

The king was so pleased with Aidan, that one day he gave him his prize possession, a magnificent horse. On the way home, however, Aidan met a beggar and gave the horse to him. The king exploded, 'My best horse! I could have given you any number of old nags to give to beggars! Why did you do it?' Aidan simply replied, 'Which is more important, my lord, the foal of a mare or a child of God?' The king was, of course, duly chastened and asked forgiveness. At this Aidan burst into tears. 'This land does not deserve a king like this,' he exclaimed. 'You will not last long in this world.' His words became prophetic, for shortly afterwards the king was murdered, and only twelve days later Aidan himself died, perhaps from a broken heart at what had happened to his close friend and associate.

Aidan was at Lindisfarne for only sixteen years, but during that time he changed the course of British Christian history. He died leaning against a buttress of a nearby church, and today that wood can be seen in Bamburgh church, although today it is set high up to prevent pilgrims and tourists taking pieces of it.

On the mainland, on the evening that Aidan died, a shepherd called Cuthbert, unaware of what was happening, saw a vision of angels taking a soul to heaven. Little did he realise that he had been chosen to assume Aidan's mantle.

Group reflections

1. Aidan was successful because he had a gentle approach. Jesus seems to have gently encouraged people with questions and stories. Share your own journey into faith and who it was who helped you the most. What lessons do you draw for your own evangelism?

2. When Jesus prayed for others, there is no evidence from the gospels that Jesus' approach to praying was ever anything but calm and specific and honoured by God. The same is true of Aidan. Give two examples of when you know your prayers for others have been answered.

3. Aidan trained local youngsters for Christian ministry. Jesus left his work to his disciples and the Holy Spirit. How is your church encouraging local people to offer Christian ministry, rather than depend on a minister?

4. Like Jesus, Aidan left a legacy of stories about how he had loved people. What are the two major stories of love that others might tell about your group?

st cuthbert of the farne islands

We have a destiny

As we read the pages of the Bible it is clear that John the Baptist was destined to prepare people for the coming of Jesus; Peter was destined to become one of the first church leaders; Mary Magdalene was destined to be the first person to see Jesus raised from the dead; and Jesus himself was destined for the cross, for resurrection and for glory. If God really is God, and if we allow him to be Lord of our life, then our own destiny will be fulfilled as well.

The youthful years

Thirteen hundred years ago a young teenage boy played near the river Tweed. He was athletic and he romped around with others of his own age. One day a three-year old child cried out, 'Cuthbert, why do you make such a fool of yourself? Do you not realize that your own nature calls you to serve God?' The youngster's words cut to the heart of Cuthbert, and this physical athlete began to change into a spiritual athlete.

One day some monks were floating logs down a river, in order to build a monastery. A great storm blew up, and some of the local peasants jeered at them because they hated this new Christian religion. Cuthbert simply knelt down on the bank and prayed. The storm ceased, and all who witnessed it realized, as we do now, that when people pray coincidences seem to happen!

Sometime later, as a shepherd, Cuthbert was near Lindisfarne looking after his sheep one night. He looked into the sky and saw a great light. He recognized angels streaming up to heaven from Lindisfarne, carrying someone's soul with them. The next day Cuthbert was told that Aidan, the prior of Lindisfarne, had died. His links with that island, and his own destiny, were beginning to unfold. It was no surprise to others when, at the age of seventeen, Cuthbert entered the monastery. When a new monastery was being built at Melrose, Cuthbert was asked to go and take on the very important task of guest master. The story runs that one winter's day it was snowing very hard. A young man called at the monastery, and after making him welcome Cuthbert went off to find some bread. But when he came back the young man had disappeared, and there were no footprints in the snow! Cuthbert came to the conclusion that he had been visited by an angel, that God indeed had drawn very near to him.

Responsibility

In AD 664 the great Synod of Whitby was held. The disappointed Celtic church leaders withdrew. Lindisfarne needed a new prior, and so at the age of just 30, Cuthbert was given this great responsibility. The first task Cuthbert had was to help the Celtic monks of Lindisfarne come to terms with the great change. They had many rows on Lindisfarne, and often Cuthbert would simply walk out of the meeting, the next day reappearing with a smile on his face as if nothing had happened.

Cuthbert became known as a responsible and wise manager. His reputation caught the imagination, and his healings became very widely known. Hundreds flocked to him, but increasingly it meant that he had no time to pray. It is said that he never left a service without tears because he was always overcome by the sense of sinfulness and of a spiritual yearning for something better.

Life as a hermit

After ten years as prior he felt worn out, and he went off to be a hermit on his own little island just to the south of Lindisfarne. If you go there today, it is a stunning, small island where there is a remarkable sense of peace. But still Cuthbert found that this was not remote enough. Still people came to him, and so he withdrew even further to one of the islands of the Inner Farnes. The first thing he did was to pray, driving the evil spirits from that island. There he built his little hut, constructed a chapel, and made a high circular wall all around his little enclosure. But still, when the tides allowed it, people came to seek his advice. He was somebody who, we are told, warmed their spirits, counselled them, lifted their burdens, and explained the wiles of the devil.

A new role

In AD 684 the area needed a new bishop. Cuthbert was asked, but he refused until both the king and other church leaders rowed out to his island and convinced him. Reluctantly he agreed, and so for two years he travelled round establishing new churches, travelling always with a limp that had been left with him from the plague.

But after two years he had to resign. He went back to the Farne Islands to die. When his monks came and found him, they discovered that he had only five onions left to eat. He gave his final instructions to the monks and died in the arms of his friends. They brought his body back to Lindisfarne, but because of the increasing Viking raids his body was carried around for many years, and in the end was interred at Durham.

The lessons?

First, he knew his life from teenage years had a purpose;

Second, he knew God's hand rested on him;

Third, and most important, Cuthbert found his own island, his Inner Farne, a symbol perhaps of the inner island he found within his own soul. He developed his relationship with God in prayer and meditation and song.

Group reflections

1. In the Old Testament Jeremiah says he felt God had his hand on his life even before he was born (Jeremiah 1.4). Cuthbert was aware of God's call early on. Looking back, can you see any overall plan of God in your life? Share it.

2. Cuthbert was initially made aware of this through a child. The Bible has many examples of children responding to God (e.g. the boy Samuel). How does your church take seriously not only the existence but the contribution of children to the spiritual direction ahead?

3. Cuthbert had a memorable experience as he offered hospitality at Melrose. Have you ever felt you were 'entertaining angels unawares' (Hebrews 13.2)?

4. Being a Christian sometimes means taking things on we would rather avoid. Cuthbert discovered this. Jesus most certainly felt this, as the account of his time in the garden of Gethsemane records. Can you offer any examples from your own life and say how God helped you through?

st hilda of whitby

A necklace of sparkling jewels

Our story begins before Hilda was born. Her parents were of royal descent, but were exiled in Yorkshire because of the violence of the age. One night her mother dreamt that she lost her husband. As she searched for him, she found a necklace sparkling with jewels amongst her clothes. In her dream she felt she was being told that the daughter she was about to bear would sparkle so brightly that she would light up the whole of this country.

Abbess of Whitby

For the first years of her life Hilda lived as a wealthy noble lady, but at the age of 33 she responded to the calling to become a nun. So in AD 657 at Whitby she built a monastery. There she developed a dual-house of both monks and nuns and her monastery became famous for its righteous mercy, purity, and charity. It is written that, 'no one possessed any goods of their own, for everything was shared, and so no one was ever in need.' The monastic community was based on three rules: justice, devotion, and chastity.

Her mind sparkled with the truth of God

Hilda developed a reputation as a wise and learned counsellor, and many flocked to her for help, including bishops and kings. Her mind was most certainly in touch with God's truth, and she was able to apply it in a practical way to peoples' lives. She became known as the 'soul-friend' of many, and was called 'mother'. In her time she trained literally hundreds of priests, five of whom in turn became bishops.

Her heart sparkled with the love of God

At Whitby today, one of the most astonishing sights is that of Caedmon's cross. It is a remarkable Celtic cross with many intricate inscriptions. Caedmon was a lay monk who was uneducated, and the story goes that one day the monks were having a feast at the end of one of their fasts. Each monk in turn had to sing a song. As the harp was passed from monk to monk, so Caedmon panicked because he did not know what to sing, so he ran into the barn, for his job was that of a cowherd. He fell asleep, and in his dream he felt that he was being told, 'You must sing.' 'I can't,' he said. 'You must', came the reply. 'What shall I sing about?' 'Sing about creation', was the response, and in his dream he sang a song. When he awoke, to his amazement, he remembered it all, and he told his steward, who in turn told Hilda.

Hilda was impressed, but wanted to test whether or not it was genuine. So she gave him another Bible passage to set to music. Beautiful music and verse was the result. Hilda immediately relieved Caedmon of all menial jobs within the monastery, so that he could be released to be the bard for everyone's benefit. There was with Caedmon a recognition that God's gift of song-writing was not just a technical gift of creating good music, but rather his songs were such that they sent the soul soaring to God. Caedmon spent time being taught the Bible, and it is written that 'he reflected on the Bible as a cow chews on the cud.' Every song that he composed was created not just in order to sound nice, but 'to turn people from their sinfulness to lives of love.'

In her monastery, Hilda encouraged the arts, poetry, music, the great patterns on crosses and on parchments, and her monastery became a great centre of literacy, a great centre of education. It was not that any of these things were ends in themselves, but they were all intended to help people be drawn further into the love and experience of God. Thus in turn they too might sparkle with the love of God, their minds might sparkle with the truth of God, and their souls might sparkle with the presence of God. There was no division for people like Hilda and Caedmon between any of those three. Is it not true that if you live in the light of God, and his light lives within you, then everything about you will sparkle with his love, even at those times when you do not feel it?

The Synod of Whitby

It was because of Hilda's great reputation that when trouble loomed in the church at large in the year AD 664, and a great synod had to be called, it was held at Whitby. It was her offer of hospitality which was accepted. In the end, the decision went against the Celtic Church, and so we have ended up today with dioceses and bishops, parish churches rather than communities, and uniform liturgies. Consequently, we have great difficulty in accommodating the charismatic, gifted people like Caedmon or their equivalent today, because they do not fit easily into the straightjacket of an organized hierarchical system.

Hilda's own choice was with the Celtic Church, so she was very disappointed at the result. The following years took their toll on her, and the strain showed. For four years she carried on her work, but then she contracted fever, probably tuberculosis, and after a further six years she died at nearby Hackness, a daughter house she had established.

Her soul sparkled with the presence of God

At Hackness a nun saw a stream of light, and angels taking her soul to heaven from Whitby. Even to the end, despite her disillusionment and illness, she never ceased to praise God. Her soul always sparkled with the presence of God.

It is comforting to know her story: that her mind sparkled with the truth of God, her heart sparkled with the love of God, and her soul sparkled with the presence of God, even to the end, and even during those days when she did not feel like it! When a diamond is mined from the ground, it is rough. It needs to be cut and honed. That is a painful job. Being shaped and polished is not pleasant. Maybe when times are particularly tough, then we too are being polished, honed and cut.

Group reflections

1. As you continue to grow in your Christian faith, what biblical passages particularly excite or 'sparkle' for you at the moment?

2. How is the 'sparkle' of artistic creativity being encouraged in your congregation at the moment – writing, music, artwork, drama . . .?

3. As you look back, name those people you have known in the past whose souls have 'sparkled with God.' What was their secret?

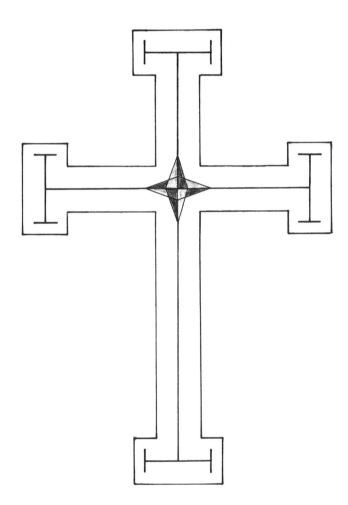

st ceóó of braówell

Reaching beyond

Visitors to Cedd's chapel at Bradwell in Essex discover that it stands at the end of a track and can only be reached on foot. It stands isolated on the edge of the coast as if reaching out to something beyond. But his story begins in Northumbria. Cedd and his three brothers were all by background Anglo-Saxon. They were adopted by Aidan into the monastery at Lindisfarne. There as young boys they were taught the Gospels, the Psalms, to read and write, and to preach, so that they could be ordained as missionary priests. What then did Cedd and his brothers do?

Reaching out to society

His first mission was among the middle-Saxons in that area known as Mercia, where he went with three colleagues. There he learnt to be an evangelist, very much 'in the saddle', watching the others and joining in as appropriate. Obviously he was very effective, for when the king of the East Saxons wanted a similar mission, it was Cedd and one other who sailed down the North Sea, in his little curragh, and found the remains of a Roman fort. There he built his monastery in AD 654. Because he was so successful, within a year he was recalled to Lindisfarne to be consecrated bishop of the East Saxons. He managed to establish Christian communities also at Mersea, Prittlewell, Upminster, and Tilbury.

The Celtic missionaries did not complicate their message. They came simply saying, in a sense, 'We see that you are reaching out to your gods with your own religion. We have come to introduce you to the God who reaches out back to you, the one who came as Jesus, who loved the world so much he was even prepared to die for us all. Just as he has given his life for you, so we invite you to give your life to him and to be baptized.' There appears to have been no threat of any sort in their message.

Reaching out to the Church

Cedd's real place in the history of this country is assured by being the interpreter at the great Synod of Whitby in AD 664. That was the great meeting where the continental approach to faith was ranged against the Celtic approach: the organized, structured, managed approach of Rome was pitted against the free, spontaneous, trusting, local approach of the Celts. Cedd was known to be on the side of Colman of Lindisfarne, but he was trusted by both sides, and he knew both Irish and Latin. In his history, Bede, writing about Cedd, likens his role to that of the Holy Spirit of Pentecost, who enabled all the different peoples from various backgrounds to understand St Peter, despite their different languages. It was exactly that which Cedd managed at Whitby.

It is amazing today that Christians of all traditions appear to find that the insights of Celtic spirituality deepen their appreciation of their own roots and backgrounds. They come together at Bradwell on common ground of a desire to travel deeper and more simply into their common heritage and the heart of God himself. Cedd's work continues!

In his own day, Cedd reached out to the whole church, hoping to bring it together. When he died of the plague in that same year, AD 664, he almost certainly died with a sense of failure because the decision went against his beloved Celtic Church. Many of its other leaders withdrew in retreat to Scotland and Ireland.

Reaching out to God

There are two particular stories that show this. The first concerns the time when he went to establish his other abbey at Lastingham, in Yorkshire. Before he laid a single stone, Bede writes that he fasted for 40 days, eating each day only some watered milk, some bread, and an egg. He spent those days praying, claiming the ground for Christ. Visitors today will still find the remains of his original abbey, with the carved patterns on the pillars, and the place where he has been buried. He most certainly did claim the ground for Christ.

The other story concerns the occasion when he met the king. The king had just visited a relation of his who was involved in an incestuous marriage. Cedd had already forbidden the king to enter that person's house, but the king ignored the command. So when Cedd met the king, he censured him, lowering his pastoral staff over him in the traditional Irish manner, warning him that his death would come at the hands of someone within his own family. That is precisely what happened.

We see from these stories Cedd travelled both the internal road of his relationship with God through prayer and fasting, and also the external road of helping himself and others to relate to God in practical living. Similarly, we too are called:

Firstly, to reach out to society with the message of salvation, a message about a God who himself reaches down to us; **secondly**, to reach out to the church with a message of love and unity, needed today as never before; **thirdly**, and perhaps most importantly, to reach out within our own souls to the God who alone can satisfy and fill us with his own very full Holy Spirit.

Group reflections

1. As you and your Christian congregation have reached out to society, name those in the past two years who have come to faith. Why do you think this is so?

2. In what ways are you reaching out to other Christian groups and denominations so that Jesus' prayer might be fulfilled that 'they might all be one' (John 17.21)?

3. Cedd prayed and fasted for 40 days just as Jesus did in the wilderness at the start of his ministry. What spiritual disciplines have you found helpful in your own Christian growth? How do you assess such growth?

practical meditations

introduction

Christians so easily divide over whether they focus on internal spiritual piety or outward acts of mission and social engagement. In fact, this divide is often the result of personality type rather than theology: am I an introvert or an extrovert? The truth is that outward engagement without deep prayer becomes just human activism with no lasting effect, while personal prayer without mission can become just self-indulgence! In reality, prayer feeds mission and mission feeds prayer.

The Celtic Christians seemed able to hold these two aspects of the Christian life in balance. They were very prayerful but also very mission-orientated, both in evangelism and in acts of charity.

The meditations that follow attempt to hold these things together, and tease out some of the practical applications that flow from an understanding of Celtic spirituality. They face up to some of the challenges facing our contemporary society, and so enable us not to make the mistake that Celtic Christianity is about retreating into a distant fantasy history!

an approach
to community

Any contemplation of Celtic knotwork releases the notion that everything in life is interwoven. We see intricate spirals and designs linking flowers, human faces, animals and angels. It is only our inner blindness that seeks to lock life into little boxes, so often creating barriers of loneliness between us as human beings; barriers of ecological disaster between us and the rest of creation; and barriers of spiritual dryness between us and God.

The Celtic Christians had a profound understanding of God:

that God has revealed himself through creation, through Jesus, and within each of us:

> God is Father, Son, and Spirit:
> therefore God is three in one
> therefore God is community.
> If we are made in the image of God
> then we will find our fulfilment when we are in community.

Monasteries

As the Celtic Christians rejected the notion of hierarchical church life, they embraced the notion of community. Adopting the pattern of the first church in Jerusalem (Acts 2 and 4), and following the example of the Desert Fathers and Mothers of Egypt and Syria, they lived in the church and went out to the world (unlike us who tend to live in the world and occasionally go to church). They drew their strength from each other in a pagan society, sharing food, money, work, play, and worship. These very simple and poor communities, often little more than a collection of stone bee-hive or wattle and daub huts around a central chapel, were the power-house of the church under the guidance of the abbot.

Not for them our approach of the 'bus-church': once a week we file in the back door, walk up the central aisle, sit in rows facing the neck of the person in front, if really fortunate we may be taken somewhere by the 'driver' at the front, half-way through the fare is collected, and at the end we file out of the back door again! That hardly allows for a time of sharing the deep things of God and how we have connected them to the events of the week.

In an age when we may know television personalities better than we know our neighbours, employ community workers to help people remember how to relate to each other, hear constantly of the elderly dying undiscovered in isolated flats, every church needs to ask how far it is incarnating the face of God (who is community) to a lonely world.

Nature

The Celtic Christians also had a profound understanding of the unity of creation. They understood that we are made of the dust of the earth and to dust we return; that if we mistreat one aspect of nature that will have a return effect on us. They would not have used terms like 'eco-system' but they knew that just as God is one, so the creation he has made is also one. Trees were only felled if necessary. In Wales, David forbade even the use of animals to pull farm implements.

One monk wrote:

> As I look out from my cave I see the wide ocean,
> Stretching west, north, and south to the ends of the earth.
> I watch the sea birds swoop and hear them shriek,
> And in my mind I can see the ocean depths teeming with fish.
> The earth is both majestic and playful, both solemn and joyful,
> And in all this, it reflects the one who made it.
>
> (Traditional)

This was not just sentimentalism, for these people lived in harsh times under harsh conditions. Rather, it was a spiritual theology which saw God in everything around. It is therefore only to be expected that many of the knotwork patterns would demonstrate the unity between vegetation, humanity and the animals.

Heaven

As well as the earthly creation, angels and saints figure not only in the patterns but also in the prayers and poems. Very often the inhabitants of heaven are not only talked *about* but talked *to*. They were seen as present in the room – as real as other human beings. As a result, it seemed natural to include them in conversations with God, as part of his company. Iona is referred to by George Macleod, founder of the Iona Community, as a 'thin place' where the distance between heaven and earth is 'tissue thin'. It is a Celtic site where heaven seems close. It is, in fact, only our lack of insight, wherever we are, which distances us from heaven – the saints and angels are all around us!

Hebrews 12 states 'we are surrounded by a great crowd of witnesses . . . let us run with determination the race that lies before us.' The image is of a Greek stadium in which all the inhabitants of heaven are the spectators in the stalls cheering us on as we run our Christian race: they are urging and willing us forward towards our goal.

There was an understanding that we are never alone – even when it seems that way. We are with nature, with each other, with the company of heaven, and with God who is himself three in one.

Group reflections

1.   How far is the 'bus church' picture true for any members of your church? (Be honest!)

2.   How far does your church reflect in practical terms the fact that 'God is community'? Read Acts 2.42-7 and Acts 4.31-5.

3.   Read Hebrews 12.1-2. How might we free our imaginations more so that we realize just how close are all the people of heaven? What might result from a true understanding of being part of the 'communion of saints'?

understanding the celtic cross

Fences, walls and hedges all declare, 'This ground is different – it belongs to me.' Centuries ago, circles of stone crosses stood like sentries around Celtic monasteries declaring 'This ground is different – it belongs to God.' In modern churches stone crosses tend to mark places of burial and death; Celtic Christians, however, marked their places of life with crosses. In doing so they were simply adopting the contemporary culture.

Culture

The Druids marked their holy places with pillars of stone or wood, often with a circle at the head carved out or scratched onto it. The circle symbolized the fact that the sun was a major divinity for them. The message of the Celtic missionaries was simple: 'We have not come to deny the importance of the sun. Indeed, without it we would have no heat, no light, no life. Rather, we have come to introduce you to the one who is behind *even* the sun, moreover has revealed himself in the person of Jesus.' Hence the pillar with the circle at its head simply developed into the Celtic cross with the arms of the cross superimposed or extending from that central orb.

Thus, when the Christian missionaries arrived they did not argue that a change of religion necessitated a change of culture – just the reverse. Indeed, they would have been horrified at the way the white western missionaries took the gospel to Africa and Asia and confused the teaching of Jesus with the culture of soap, western dress, and European language! Only in this century have contextualization and inculturation been rightly understood within mission. Even in this country, the church is still grappling with a predominantly middle-class institution seeking to share God's love among Urban Priority Areas, where particular styles of language, management, worship and forward planning are simply inappropriate.

Often, Druid holy sites were adopted and simply Christianized. The place where a holy man lived would now be the base for a Christian hermit. Where local people gathered for Druid rites would become the gathering place for Christian worship. The cross instead of the pillar would mark the place. Just as Jesus said to the Jews, 'I have come not to destroy, but to fulfil the law and the prophets' (Matthew 5.17), so the Celtic missionaries made it clear they had come to fulfil the pre-Christian hopes – not destroy them.

Places

Some of these crosses were twenty feet high. Technically the circle helps to support the horizontal arms, and often they would be placed to mark a spot where a significant event had taken place – a battle won by a Christian king, a dramatic healing or miracle, or a place devoted to a holy person, such as where Columba used to rest on Iona.

There were few priests and churches then, and the clergy tended to have a wandering teaching and evangelistic ministry. They would simply 'set up their stall' at a natural meeting place and set up a cross as they met with success. As culture was enfolded rather than confronted, and people converted, so place-names evolved – Crossthwaite, Crossdale, Waltham Cross. Rather like blue plaques today mark the site of the home of a famous person or the site of a significant occurrence, so those markers fulfilled that function – but more than that.

Teaching

These crosses were often highly decorated with biblical teaching. One side might be full of Old Testament scenes foreshadowing Jesus: Adam and Eve (the fall requiring a saviour), Noah (offering salvation from a wicked world), Abraham and Isaac (a father ready to sacrifice his son), and David and Goliath (the hero battling on behalf of his people against the enemy). The other side might often have New Testament scenes, especially of the crucifixion, Pilate washing his hands, the empty cross of the resurrection, Jesus in glory in heaven, and the Last Judgement.

They were pictorial visual aids in a non-literate age, no different today to the use of videos, overhead projectors and computer games to teach Christian truths. It is simply an extension of the educational genius Jesus made use of with parables as visual stories, active miracles as demonstrations, and bread and wine as tangible symbols.

Prayer

Above all, these crosses were not meant to be quaint monuments, but aids to prayer drawing travellers into the mysteries of God. They spoke of the creator behind even the sun, of Jesus who hung on the cross, of Creation shot through with redemption. They spoke of an enfolding approach to mission and of the stories of the Old and the New Testament. They invited the traveller to pause and consider, to reflect on life and on God, to spend time in prayer and adoration, and to leave feeling different because of that time spent at a holy place – perhaps more determined to make other places holy. 'The time is coming,' said Jesus, 'when you will worship the Father neither on this mountain nor in Jerusalem . . . but in spirit and in truth' (John 4) – in other words, everywhere! For if the Spirit is within you, that place where you are becomes holy, touched by a holy person.

Group reflections

1. Jesus came as a Jew to the Jewish people but also crossed cultural boundaries by speaking to Samaritans and women; he touched lepers and befriended prostitutes; and in the Gospels he engaged with Greeks and Romans as well as Jews. What cultural boundaries are you crossing in Christian mission?

2. What cultural boundaries have to be crossed by anyone joining a church in terms of social grouping, music, language, etc?

3. How might it be possible today to mark places where people have been healed, called, or have made an important Christian commitment?

4. What are the cultural icons of today? How might they be adapted to convey Christian truth?

the pilgrimage of life

Pilgrimage is fashionable again today. Hundreds of thousands travel to the ancient Celtic sites of Iona, Lindisfarne and Whithorn, and it features in the RE National Curriculum for schools.

Originally from Southern and Central Europe, by 300 BC the Celts were the dominant race in Europe. For those seeking biblical connections, as with the name 'Gaul', 'Galatia' derives from the same root-word as 'Celt', so Paul's letter to the Galatians was written to the dominant tribe in Turkey at that time – the Celts! They seem to have been driven by a human urge always to move on physically. This was later matched, as their soul were fired by the Christian faith, to make an inner spiritual journey at the same time. These two urges became wonderfully harnessed to create the great evangelistic thrust of the Celtic churches.

The way

They easily understood the biblical assertion that 'here we have no abiding city' (Hebrews 13). They knew Jesus not as the *answer* or the *destination*, but rather as 'the *way*, the truth and the life' (John 14), the one who described himself as both the 'alpha and the omega – the beginning and the end' (Revelation 1). Life was seen as a journey in which the outer body and the inner soul sustain each other. We move on always to discover more of God rather than to find God. As one monk wrote with great insight in the tenth century:

> To go to Rome is of much trouble, little profit,
> For the king whom you seek,
> Unless you bring him with you
> You will not find.
>
> (Traditional)

They loved the biblical stories of the great travellers – Abraham, Noah, Moses, and even Jonah the reluctant pilgrim! These characters they carved onto their high crosses. They understood that these people already knew God but set out on an adventure to discover even more of him. Their physical journeys matched their spiritual journeys.

The destination

Many of us have a repetitive life, perhaps always being at the same place each week on the same day – Monday morning at work, Tuesday evening at a club, Sunday at church, and so on. But because of the events of the intervening days, we are not the same people we were the previous week. We have moved on, crossing and re-crossing the same point, rather like the patterns in the knotwork. Jesus is the 'alpha and the omega' – the beginning and the end may be the same point. As important as those beginning and end points is the 'Way' in between – for Jesus is also 'the way' (John 14). We discover that, in fact, the *destination* is the journey itself.

It is always better to travel hopefully than to arrive. Once we think we have 'arrived,' our souls have died. We can never say 'I have grown sufficiently as a Christian disciple', nor can we keep relying on experiences or insights or revelations of twenty years ago. It is only the reality of our present spiritual journey that gives any credibility to our witness.

Celtic monks often set off with no set destination in mind, simply travelling, as one wrote, 'for the love of God, for the name of Christ, and for the salvation of souls.' They travelled on foot rather than horseback so that it was easy to stop and share their faith with those they met. In contrast to our attitude to journeys with timetables, luggage, and speed, they would savour the journey, enjoy the views, talk with others, pray as they went, and share their faith.

In AD 891 three Irish monks drifted for seven days at sea, landing in Cornwall. When challenged by King Alfred they said 'we stole away because we wanted for the love of God to be on pilgrimage, we cared not where.' These perpetual wanderers left everything to go into the unknown to discover more of creation and more of themselves. As they did so, both the transcendent God 'beyond' and the imminent God 'within' were being met. The journey was a sacrament, 'an outward and visible sign of an inner and spiritual grace.' Leaving all human props and shackles behind, both they and those they met discovered the secrets of spiritual growth.

Penance

Esther de Waal in *A World Made Whole* outlines three types of Celtic martyrdom:

> Red martyrdom: separation from the soul at death (martyrdom by sword or fire was very rare in the Celtic churches);
>
> Green martyrdom: separated from one's desires (penance as a spiritual exercise was widely practised);
>
> White martyrdom: separated from one's beloved homeland (self-imposed exile was common and very painful for these home-lovers).

Such journeys, then, were not luxury holidays, but spiritual disciplines, and as Brendan sailed the Atlantic, Columbanus travelled to Italy, others even to Russia and Iceland, so evangelism was effected as Ninian, Patrick, Columba, Aidan, Cuthbert, Chad, Cedd and a host of others were all gripped by this insatiable wanderlust that forbade them to stay still even though they were great home-lovers.

Group reflections

1. In Acts 9.2 Christians are called 'followers of the Way of the Lord.' Share how your life at the moment is part of a journey deeper into the heart of God. What are you learning that grips you at present?

2. Jesus 'had nowhere to lay his head.' Are there ways in which Christians might travel more light of material possessions?

3.   How might we develop the ability to allow each external experience to be a revelation of God to our internal souls?

4.   What steps could we take to make travelling simply more enjoyable?

5.   What 'holy' sites would you want to visit and why? What is the difference between being a pilgrim and a tourist?

the community
of nature

Columbanus wrote, 'If you wish to understand the Creator, then first understand his creation' In other words, the way to understand the mind of an artist is through his picture, a potter through her pottery, an author through her writing, and so on. The Celtic missionaries saw God as the master craftsman who sculpted the mountains, painted the sunset, engineered the storm, stirred the sea. They did not pretend to understand scientifically, but intuitively and emotionally knew that nature belongs to God.

Today with horror we use phrases like ozone layer, greenhouse gases, genetic breeding, factory farming, deforestation. Scientifically we have begun to understand the oneness of nature, that to abuse one area will affect a whole chain of events, and we are learning that we cannot behave as though nature is ours to pillage. The Celtic missionaries went with the flow of nature, working with the cycle of the days and nights, the seasons, the tides and the weather. They respected the Druids' sacred groves, refused to fell trees unnecessarily, and revered sacred wells.

Then there was an understanding that in the Genesis story of Creation when humanity is told to have dominion over the earth, that authority was to be exercised in the same way as Jesus exercises his dominion (lordship) over the church – in selfless service and sacrifice, giving himself for the sake of the church. Today's approach of planting a new tree for each one felled would have gained approval from the Celts.

As 'Adam' means 'red earth', reminding us that we come from and return to the same source as every other living thing, so the Celtic Christians understood that 'humanity' is meant to show 'humility' before the 'humus', or earth, from which we come. There are many legends about the Celtic saints demonstrating this sense of oneness with nature:

In Ireland, **Cieren** enjoyed the aid of a wild boar which used its tusks to help dig the foundations of his hut, and when Cieren died, he asked that he might be laid beside his hut on the green turf, facing his beloved sky.

Kevin, again in Ireland, was one day lost in meditation and rested his arm on a ledge. He was still for so long that a blackbird not only rested on his fingers but built a nest in his hand. Furthermore, Kevin was still for so long that the blackbird not only laid eggs in the nest, but the eggs were able to hatch and the birds fly away! Sometime later, when Kevin wanted to take Christianity to a neighbouring village but was unsure how to proceed, a cow came to him. The cow later returned to the village and produced twice as much milk as usual. The same thing happened the next day. On the third day the villagers followed the cow, discovered Kevin, and, of course, all became Christians!

We read that when **Columba** was on Iona dying, his horse laid its head on his lap crying. A stag helped **Cainech** to read the scriptures apparently by using his antlers to keep the pages open!

On Lindisfarne, **Colman** had three pets: a cockerel who would wake him up at midnight if he failed to rise for prayer; a mouse who rested on his shoulder and would nibble his ear if he slept for more than five hours without praying; and a fly who would crawl along the page as he was reading the scriptures, stopping if Colman paused to meditate, thereby reminding him of his place on the page!

Again on Lindisfarne, we read of **Cuthbert** having his feet dried by two otters as he came out of the North Sea after praying all night.

In Ireland, **Brigid** heard about the village fool who had killed a tame fox belonging to the king. The king was so enraged that he vowed the fool would die. Brigid raced to help, praying as she went. As she rushed off, into her chariot jumped another tame fox which she was able to give to the king and, of course, everyone lived happily ever after!

No-one believes all these tales, but they are meant to be *stories with a truth*. They hint at a desire to fulfil the Messianic prophecy in Isaiah 11 that the 'wolf and the lamb will lie down together'. They hint at a recovery of that closeness Jesus had with the animals when at his temptation in the wilderness no wild beasts harmed him. The Old Testament speaks of the floods clapping their hands, the mountains leaping for joy and the trees reaching up in praise. Jesus who rode on a donkey on Palm Sunday exclaimed that even the stones could cry out proclaiming his presence if the crowds were silenced. At the crucifixion there was an earthquake and an eclipse as the life of the Creator hung by a thread.

Much of this may be pictorial language or reflection after the event, but it speaks of a unity in creation. It is a far cry from experiments on animals in an attempt to improve our cosmetics, exploiting calves to obtain whiter meat, removing vast tracts of forest simply to provide ourselves with unnecessary wrapping paper, draining oil from the ground to pollute the atmosphere with car engines, cancer caused by a combination of stress and the sun's rays, asthma resulting from industrial pollution, diseases that cross species through cheap feeding methods, and oil-slicks that destroy sea-life.

The Celtic Christians would have been very near to calls for recycling, fighting for animal rights, campaigning on environmental issues, vegetarian diets, and near to those who work with Traidcraft, buying and selling fairly.

Group reflections

1. What factors prevent us adopting ecologically friendly purchasing policies in our homes, churches or places of work? Are these reasons or excuses? What could be done?

2. Are there groups we should be lobbying on environmental issues?

3. Do the lifestyles of the Celtic saints suggest any issues to be addressed in our eating habits and diets?

4. What are the implications of all this for 'church social functions' if Christians are meant to be the Messianic community showing a foretaste of God's ideal?

holy times and places

The ancient Celts and the Jews shared many similarities: both believed in an after-life, in angels and demons, good and evil, and in a distinct code of morality. Both measured their effective day, not as we do from morning to evening, but rather from sunset to sunset (hence in Genesis we read, 'There was evening and morning, the first day'. Similarly, their New Year began with the onset of winter. Consequently, Christianity was seen to fulfil the Druidic religion just as naturally as it had the Jewish faith, and customs were easily adopted and assimilated.

Times

The Druids based their understanding of the year around the solstices and equinoxes, when the sun is furthest from the equator and when it crosses the equator.

Samhein (1 November) opened the agricultural calendar with a well-deserved rest for the land, and when death seems nearest. It is a 'thin' time of the year when the elderly and frail may die. Those cattle clearly unable to survive the winter were killed, their meat eaten and the carcasses thrown onto the 'bone-fire'. Sacrifices were made to the gods, and spirits came up from beneath the ground and beyond this life. The Celtic natural feel for this survives still.

Although 5 November has a different rationale, we still light 'bonfires' at that season (long after the historical reason has disappeared). We celebrate All Souls and All Saints days that same month. Halloween gives evil spirits their last chance before the light of Christ dawns. Although fewer now personally remember the First World War, Remembrance Day with its sense of communion with the departed is still important. At that time of year, time and eternity seem to meet, and it is natural to reflect on mortality, the afterlife, and ancient customs and wisdom. To accept this as a fact of life is a very Celtic thing to do: it is simply going with the natural flow of life.

Imbolc began on 1 February when the earth begins to wake up and the days lengthen. This was Christianized into St Brigid's Day and became a great festival of light.

Beltain, 1 May, heralded a time of merrymaking and welcoming of summer, and significantly this survives as May Day. It is at this time that now we hold Rogation Tide services blessing the crops, and the animals as they are driven back to the hills.

Lughnasa, 1 August, was the time for weddings and fertility, when prayers were said for the crops as they were harvested. In time this developed into the Christian festival of Lammas, when the first wheat gathered would be made into a communion loaf.

This 'going with the flow' and making times into holy occasions, challenges us to dedicate the natural rhythm of our lives to God. We make the ordinary cycle of events into holy times as we do simple things like pray as we wake, as we dress, as we eat, as we work, as we go to sleep. It is about praying with a natural rhythm in our spirituality. It also challenges us to reorder our Christian year to fit comfortably with the natural year. For example, the Celtic Christians stayed in during the cold months to pray and study, and went out evangelising in the summer. Today, most churches seem to collapse during the summer months when people may be at their most relaxed and receptive!

Places

The same principle was true for places as it was for time – 'fulfil not destroy' what already exists was the Celtic maxim, drawing on Jesus' approach with his Jewish contemporaries. Iona was adopted as a base by Columba because it was already a Druid holy site. As Druid schools became Christian so they often simply re-formed into monasteries. Christian hermits often based themselves by already sacred wells, now simply telling Christian instead of pagan stories. There was a recognition that wells were sources of life (fresh water), places of healing (often simply a clean bath!), and a place of entry into the nether-world where spirits lived and were to be placated with offerings (today we not only still throw coins into wells but we create them specially in modern shopping malls!). In the Peak District well-dressing continues using clay and flower petals to portray local or biblical scenes.

As Abraham, Joshua and Moses all built stone cairns and altars to designate sites of special revelation or experience of God, so the Celtic Christian followed suit. Crosses were erected, as with the remarkable tall cross at Ruthwell. Wells were dedicated, as at Chadwell Heath near Romford (probably by Cedd in honour of his brother Chad). Ground was claimed as holy by Cedd at Lastingham, where he fasted for 40 days before building his monastery. It should come as no surprise that these ancient Celtic sites still draw thousands, despite the fact that they are often very difficult to reach.

Group reflections

1. Outline the pattern of your day and week. How far does it go with the natural flow of light and darkness, heat and cold? What effect does our present pattern of living have on our bodies and souls?

2. Jesus began his ministry with the words, 'The time has come' (Mark 1.15). This did not mean chronological time, but rather the 'occasion' has arrived. What have been the three most special 'moments' in your life? Would you call them holy?

3. During the Exodus the wandering Israelites marked special places with altars. In Scotland cairns perform a similar function. What places would you want to mark as having been very special to you? Would you call them holy?

4. What do you think it is that makes some places seem quite special, while others can have quite a negative atmosphere?

5. What could you do to make your home a holy place where holy occasions happen? What might such phrases mean about your home?

on the road

Today's commuters know all about road rage, congestion and traffic fumes. Most journeys seem to be functional rather than enjoyable. We try to get from A to B as quickly as possible because it is the destination that is important, while the journey itself is simply a necessary aggravation. Celtic travellers were very different!

The Celtic saints had journeying in their blood. Columbanus, for example, travelled from Ireland to Rome setting up monasteries. Columba did not settle until he reached Iona. Brendan sailed across the Atlantic even to America. For 500 years a constant stream of Irish Christians took the light of Christ to the Continent and beyond.

An experience of God

Columbanus wrote, 'I am always moving, from the day of my birth to the day of my death. Christians must travel in perpetual pilgrimage as guests of this world.' When asked by the Pope why he was establishing a Celtic monastery just twenty miles from Rome, he explained that travelling through the world was symbolic of the travelling within his soul: travelling physically enabled him to experience God, both intellectually and emotionally, as well as spiritually.

As we travel, so we can let our imagination run riot: the hills and valleys show us God the sculptor; the sky and clouds show us God the artist; the stars point us to God the physicist; each person we meet enables us to see something of the personal image of God. The sheer drama of a storm or the splendour of mountains and waterfalls is meant to make us feel over-awed! God has given us hearts full of feeling so that travelling through apparently impersonal scenery becomes a highly personal reflection on the Creator.

It may be that as we travel, we listen to a tape of Christian music or teaching. It may be that it is alone in the car we can pray aloud, simply letting the surroundings speak to us of God. Even in towns we need not react negatively. To be stuck in queue beside a bus can be a spring-board for meditation: 'Lord, the bus tyre connects the bus to the road, just as Jesus connected God to heaven; the tyre gets worn and abused and eventually thrown away in making that connection, just as Jesus did . . .' – even a bus tyre can be a source for meditation! That is thoroughly Celtic in approach.

An opportunity for mission

Today we tend to fear talking on a journey! Maybe it is 'British stiff upper lip', maybe we are embarrassed to share our faith, maybe we fear the reaction we might incur simply through talking to a stranger! Celtic bishops, however, were always on foot, never on horseback, in order to enable easy conversation with fellow travellers. Celtic travellers often left communities of Christian believers in their wake.

Celtic missionaries travelled chattering to those they met, striking up relationships, sharing their faith, and remaining as friends – it was not confrontational but natural. Too many of us today, it seems, treat our religion like going to the toilet – something we deal with in private and never talk about!

Aidan of Lindisfarne gave away a beautiful horse to a beggar as a sign of the bounty of God – actions speaking louder than words. One RAF chaplain had a rule always to give loose change to buskers. As we travelled once in London and passed a dozen or so in one journey, so he commented, 'I'm almost out of change – it'll have to be notes now!' What a wonderfully Jesus-like approach to travelling, and certainly very Celtic.

Claiming the land

Different places do give off different 'vibes': one area can seem very friendly and relaxed, another full of gossip or fear, or depression. Yet while these atmospheres can be very real and make a huge difference to the people living there, these descriptions never figure in estate agents' descriptions! Yet the *feel* of a place is what can make all the difference. Evangelism is not just about sharing our faith with people, it is about affecting the very ground people live on. When Cuthbert left Lindisfarne for the Inner Farne Islands, it was believed they were full of demons. Cuthbert prayed that all evil forces should be cast right away. Certainly, today these islands are amazing places of rest and peace.

Romans 8 and Ephesians 1 speak of 'powers and principalities' that can take control of people and places – and this is true also for buildings – even churches. Some churches are relaxed and easy places where faith grows, people are converted and healing happens. But other churches have such a history of intrigue and bitterness and division that evil seems to have eaten into the very fibre of the place, and so it is not surprising when we hear they are rarely used for anything other than Sunday services, even then things rarely seem to take off spiritually. As we travel through a place we can pray for that area or those buildings. We may be the only people that ever do! As we pray so we open a curtain in the window of heaven and allow something of the light of God to stream through. Celtic Christians would erect and leave behind them a wooden or stone cross. We can hardly do that today, but we can still claim the place for God.

Group reflections

1. Discuss what you have seen on your journeys this week. How might any of those scenes reveal something of God for you? Be imaginative!

2. Read John 4.1-42. What does this passage tell us about how to use situations we encounter on our travels in an evangelistic way?

3. Read Romans 8.37-9. How would you describe the spiritual atmosphere of your neighbourhood? Is it conducive to experiencing the power and love of God or is that difficult? How might you 'claim the ground' for God?

at work

Work today can be characterised by fear of redundancy, fear of lagging behind in the skills market, or a realisation that life on Benefit may be more lucrative. Some have to work 60 hours a week simply to keep their job, while others exist on short-term or zero-hours contracts. Certainly, fewer people are working longer hours to produce more, and for them it can feel reminiscent of the plight of the Hebrew slaves in Egypt who had to produce more bricks with less straw! So within that real human situation, what godly witness can we bring to bear beyond the simple, 'I must not steal paper clips, and I must tell others I go to church.' We know that at one end of the spectrum becoming a missionary appears to be very *godly*, while to be a hired assassin appears very *godless*. In reality, however, most people are somewhere in between and have to face much more searching issues. The Celtic Christians pose us three questions:

1.   Where are we going in our work?

Celtic Christians understood life to be a pilgrimage, and the knotwork patterns are a reminder that while we may emerge back at the same place, the same desk, every Monday morning, in fact we will be different because of what we have experienced since last week. In this travelling, we travel always with God. It is the travelling that is important, not the destination, because the *destination is in fact the journey itself*!

That suggests that a work-goal of, 'I want to be on the top floor with the biggest desk and the deepest carpet' misses the point. It is not about taking on a task because it will look good on our cv. The real question is, 'Where am I going in my soul at work?'

Consider ambition. Jesus gave up the glory of the board-room of heaven to come down the ladder to the shop-floor of earth. He actively took demotion to do his Father's will. Similarly, the Celtic churches were not obsessed with hierarchy. The bishops were often farm labourers in the monastery. They were chosen simply because it was seen that in their jobs they travelled with God. 'Where am I going in my job?' is not a question about promotion. It is about seeing the job as a vocation: 'Is this the job *God* wants me to do? How does it fit into *his* scheme of things?' The accountant who understands her job as creating order out of chaos in the jumbled figures on the pages, is reflecting God the creator. The despatch rider who understands his job as reflecting God the communicator, has understood the nature of vocation. Christian vocations are not just limited to clergy, nurses and teachers!

2.   How do we reflect the nature of God at work?

The Celtic Christians understood that God is creator and saviour and sustainer – Father, Son and Spirit. He is three-in-one. He is community. He is togetherness, solidarity. Yet in order to be efficient at work so often those in authority feed on the individual – the fear of the individual employee terrified of losing his job, and the greed of the individual shareholder. Economic growth is the goal and the god! However, whenever the Celtic monasteries were given any money, it was used simply to give the poor food, clothing, shelter or to buy freedom from slavery. It was all given out so that the standard of living of others might be raised and so enable them to experience something of the bounty of God. Material solidarity was the order of the day. Today this would substantially affect our attitude to pay rises, taxation and support for those not in work or in poorly paid employment! It also has implications if we discover we are part of a system that is exploiting others unjustly.

Issues of solidarity will force us to notice how far we encourage togetherness in the work place: do we continue the prejudices about 'us and them' between those on the shop floor, in the offices, or out on the road? In the canteen do management and juniors sit together or separately? How far are we working to reflect the fact of God, who is community?

3.   How do we relate work and prayer?

Celtic monasteries worked according to a sense of rhythm. Reflecting the turn of the seasons, the tides, the night and the day, so those working in the fields or copying scriptures would stop to pray at least at dawn and noon and dusk. Saturday was observed as a day of rest (the Jewish Sabbath), and one year in seven the fields lay fallow. Columba's monastery was described as being 'filled with prayer and study and manual work, in the dairy, in the granary, in the field, and each one worshipped God in their appropriate tasks and made their toil sacramental.' Their work was a sign of the presence of God. They would pray as they milked the cows, dug the earth, washed the clothes, and usually in a very trinitarian way. A modern example of this from the setting of an office is given above in the section *How to compose a Celtic blessing* (p.78).

As Cedd prayed over the stones he used to build his monastery at Lastingham, so we can pray over our paperwork, our car units on the production line, or the packages waiting to be delivered. As Muslims will stop at work today to roll out their prayer mats at set times of the day, so there is a lesson here for Christians. For example, those working with a VDU all day need to focus their eyes away from the screen every fifteen minutes, and perhaps that is the time to offer a short prayer.

The Celtic knotwork patterns show that everything is connected – plants, animals, people, angels and God – and that includes the bank, the prison, the hospital, the garage, the office. If those early monks were producing these patterns today, as well as caricatured birds and people they would include cartoon caricatures of cars, laboratory equipment and microchips! They would encourage us to be aware that God is as present at work as he is in the church.

Group reflections

1.   If God was to ask how your daily occupation fitted in with his divine plan for creation, how would you answer?

2. Moses confronted Pharaoh on behalf of the Israelite workers, at some considerable personal risk. Would you ever consider confronting your boss on behalf of others at work?

3. The fishermen Simon and Andrew, James and John met Jesus while working. How might you develop the art of recognising how the Lord is with you at work?

at home

Ancient Celtic Christian homes were draughty huts with smoky fires, earthen floors and very basic. What could they possibly offer our double-glazed, carpeted, centrally heated homes full of modern appliances? Curiously, it is often those homes which are materially the most full that are, in fact, the most empty. Modern houses have been described as 'an arrangement of beds around a microwave!' A family home may simply be a house where people fail to relate to each other, and take refuge in their own rooms each with its own television or computer screen. A home for an older person may simply be a house where an isolated person dies unnoticed. So how do we ensure that our homes represent not the worst of earth, but the best of heaven?

Places of prayer

In the last century Alexander Carmichael travelled the Hebridean Islands collecting Celtic prayers and poems which we can still enjoy in his book, the *Carmina Gadelica*. Amongst them are domestic prayers which make it clear these folk prayed as they went about their ordinary household tasks – washing, sweeping, collecting the milk, making cheese, digging the peat, sewing clothes and making bread. Not that this was a romantic rural life! Subsistence-living on the edge of the Atlantic doing back-breaking jobs was hard. Yet in the ordinary they celebrated the presence of God.

Today, in order to demean some women, ask 'What do you do for a living?' Then see if the apologetic answer is, 'I'm *just* a housewife!' To embarrass a man, catch him with a duster in his hand. Vacuuming or washing up is seldom enjoyable, yet a modern example of such praying, which can transform the most menial task is:

> As I do the washing up, Lord,
> Wash me with compassion,
> Wash me with kindness,
> Wash me with humility,
> Wash me with gentleness,
> And wash me with patience.

(Source: unknown)

It is, surely, as our homes become known as places of prayer that they take on a new significance. It is as married couples pray together, as children are prayed with, as visitors share prayers over the kitchen table that we begin to understand why Cuthbert on the Farne Islands had so many visitors – his simple home was not luxurious, but it was attractive as a place where the resident was simply God.

Places of hospitality

The Celtic Christians looked to St John for their inspiration of discipleship: St John who obeyed Jesus' last request on the cross to care for his mother, Mary – presumably in his home.

In Wales, David's huge monastery kept hot food for guests despite his own monks living only on bread and water. Before he went to Iona, Columba's monastery in Derry fed up to 1,000 callers each day. At Melrose, Cuthbert had the important job of guest-master. In Ireland, the rule at Brigid's monastery was that one twelfth of everything had to be kept for visitors. They seemed to understand the passage in Hebrews 13 which speaks of welcoming guests, for in doing so we may be 'entertaining angels unawares.'

While we clearly need to be careful about unknown visitors these days, we have here an attitude far removed from, 'My home is my castle'. Perhaps it is about simply offering a thermos of tea to the new people moving in next door, inviting neighbours in for a cuppa, asking folk for dinner with no expectation of a return meal. That is a reflection of the kingdom of heaven which Jesus so often described as a banquet with open doors.

In-between places

These Celtic monasteries, collections of simple Christian homes, were often 'open prisons' providing sanctuary for the refugee, banks where valuables could be deposited in trust, and places which were *different*. They were places where there was a little glimpse of heaven – an 'in-between place'. When others entered the gate, they were entering some small experience of heaven – a place where Jesus was Lord.

We may live as the sole Christian in our home, and feel unable to make a real difference to the atmosphere there. If that is the case, we should never underestimate the influence we have. We are *not* alone, in fact: we have the Father and the Son and the Spirit and all his angels! Celtic Christians were very aware of that.

We may live with other Christians at home (not necessarily easy!), or we may live alone. Whatever our situation we can work at creating a home where we can say to those who call at the door, 'Do come in, because in my home you will experience something of heaven because *I* live here. And because *I* live here, the God who lives in me lives here. And because God lives here, this is an 'in-between place' – a place where something of heaven can be experienced!'

Group reflections

1. Why do you think it is that praying beside each other in church is acceptable, while praying together at home is so difficult for so many Christians? How might you tackle this?

2. Read Matthew 11.19. Jesus clearly made a priority of enjoying meals with those normally excluded from polite circles. Who are the equivalent people today in your community to whom you might offer friendship, an open door or a meal?

3. Read Luke 19.1-10. When Jesus entered the home of Zacchaeus things changed. What three practical steps might you take to ensure your home increasingly is a reflection of the kingdom of heaven?

Between Friends

Who is *your* best friend? The author of Ecclesiastes wrote, 'a faithful friend is the medicine of life.' Do you eat and drink together, shop together, holiday together? Do you share hopes and fears, and, most important of all, do you share your internal spiritual journey together? Celtic Christians understood that God is Father and Son and Spirit: God is three-in-one: God is *community*. Consequently they lived together in their Celtic monasteries as communities – reflecting the nature of God. Each would have had at least one 'soul-friend'. Often in smaller monasteries it would be the abbot. The role was so vital that Jesus was called the 'Abbot of heaven'. Indeed, one monk wrote, 'a person with no soul-friend is like a person with no head' ('a headless chicken' we might say!). He would not lord it over the others, but stand beside to help them think things through before decisions were made. As monasteries grew so it became too much for one person and the role became shared among many.

The Desert Fathers and Mothers, on whom the Celts based their vision, each appointed to every monk a **syncellus** – one who shared a cell with you (both the physical cell and the inner cell of the heart). The Celtic word was **anamchara**: a person to confide in, who was warm and accepting, reliable and patient, honest and vulnerable, who might say uncomfortable words if necessary, who could be trusted, who would love you, who genuinely tried to live a holy life, and who knew the scriptures. In today's increasingly mobile society when people have to pay for counsellors and therapists, it is even more important to find a soul-friend. The extended family with the nearby wise old aunt has gone, homes split more readily, and friends move away. With whom do we reflect the nature of God – community – and share our deepest yearnings?

Examples

When the Celtic bishops wanted to know if Augustine really was a man of God, they enquired of a 'wise one' – an anamchara. When Columbanus wanted to know how to escape the advances of young women, an anamchara told him he would have to keep on the move all his days. This he did! Patrick, Columba and Brigid all visited their anamchara who could 'see' into their souls. Indeed, Columba's exile to Iona was only undertaken on the advice of an anamchara. Herbert on Derwentwater and Cuthbert on Lindisfarne were so close as soul-friends that they died on the same day even though on opposite sides of the country! Brigid was the soul-friend of many bishops and kings who came to her for advice. Aidan was the king's soul-friend at Bamburgh, advising him how to respond to the needs of the poor with generosity. Cedd was the soul-friend of the king of the East-Saxons, able to reprimand him for entering the home of a relative involved in an incestuous relationship. Today, the Community of Aidan and Hilda insists that members have soul-friends, and meet regularly as part of a disciplined life – a release not a burden.

Disciplined friendships

Such a relationship involves being unafraid to ask, 'How is your walk with God going?' 'What new thing has God taught you recently?' 'What have you learned from the Scriptures this month?' 'How are you growing in generosity, love and patience?' 'How are you exercising the Gifts of the Spirit?'

Discipline was central. There are many examples of Celtic penitentiaries, especially from Ireland. These are complete manuals covering every possible sin and the penance imposed by the soul-friend. Usually they involved doing exactly the opposite of the sin confessed; e.g. for being greedy the penance was bread and water for a week; for gossip it was silence for a week. For some quite unmentionable sin, one of the worst involved being chained to a corpse in a cave for a week!

The notion was *not* that of the law-court: these were not fines to pay God for breaking his law. Rather, the Celtic model was that of the health centre: it was medicine to help healing by focusing the mind away from the problem. As one monk wrote, 'As the floor is swept each day, so is the soul.'

Mutual need

Our own spiritual coming to faith may have been quick, but our growth is most certainly slow. None of us can do it alone: we are built for community not isolated individualism. If we have no soul-friend it may be through pride (who can possibly help *me*?) or fear (I dare not expose *my* inadequacies!). In either case, a soul-friend is needed to help moving on in the spiritual life!

How do we find a person who will pray for and with us, be a role model yet be beside us, be a coach and mentor, who will suggest what we may not wish to hear, and above all, who will help our souls soar to heaven? For the vast majority, the extraordinary fact is that God usually already has placed the very person under our noses, but who probably seems so ordinary that we haven't considered them as an anamchara! It is precisely about that Celtic business of finding the extraordinary in the ordinary!

If we wish to find a soul-friend, the best way is surely to become one ourselves – not to lord it over others, but to be ready to be open and vulnerable, to put our life in the hands of others. As in the Bible Moses and Joshua, David and Jonathan, and Paul and Barnabas had that sort of honest relationship, so Jesus was the soul-friend to his disciples. It involved risk and finally led to crucifixion as his friends proved unreliable – but ultimately it meant resurrection. Vulnerability in friendship is crucial. That is the Celtic approach, based on Jesus himself.

Group reflections

1. Read 1 Samuel 20. David and Jonathan clearly shared a very deep friendship which included a dependence on God. Why do we often find it difficult to offer such friendship?

2. What are the consequences of trying to develop our inner spiritual lives alone?

3. How could the notion of 'soul-friends' be developed in your church?

with the land

A catechism attributed to Ninian includes the lines:

Q   What is the best thing in the world?

A   To do the will of our maker.

Q   What is his will?

A   That we should live according to the laws of his creation.

Q   How do we know those laws?

A   By studying the Scriptures with devotion.

Q   What tool has our maker provided for this study?

A   The intellect, which can probe everything.

Q   What is the fruit of this study?

A   To perceive the eternal word of God, reflected in every plant and insect, every bird and animal, and in every man and woman.

Celtic Christians were holistic: they understood that everything was connected. Their knot-work patterns demonstrated the unity of the birds, plants, animals, people and angels. They would be amazed to discover that it is only recently we have woken up to the fact that our dependence on the motor car results in rising asthma in children, that destroying forests affects the global temperature, and polluting rivers affects the food we eat. As God the Father sends the Son who gave the Spirit who brings us to the Father, so that unity is reflected in creation. A trinitarian approach to the land is helpful.

Caring for the creation of the Father

The word 'Druid' comes from *Drus* meaning oak. Druids wrote using Ogham, a tree alphabet. Their shrines were made of wood, sacred material, but trees were honoured and never cut needlessly. The Celtic Christian missionaries easily built on this centrality of trees. They carved on their high crosses pictures of the tree in the garden of Eden (symbolizing the fall), the tree of the cross (symbolizing salvation), the tree of life in Revelation (symbolizing heaven), and so summarized the whole gospel. They spoke of a God who loved his creation so much that he became part of it in his incarnation.

In Ireland when the saintly Brigid prayed for the crops or the herds, their fruitfulness increased dramatically. When explaining the gospel to a dying king she wove a cross from reeds. Through the centuries these crosses have been made and hung in people's homes. Each year a new one is made and the old one is hung in the barn, and the following year it is ploughed into the field. It is all a symbol of asking God's blessing on the whole of life – the home, the animals, the crops. That cannot be done with 'unsaintly' hands, of course. It means that today, if we leave litter, dogs' mess, send junk mail, refuse to share transport or buy eco-friendly goods, then to pray for such blessing risks the charge of hypocrisy. Within the church's year there is a case for suggesting that Rogation Sunday prayers should only happen where farms pursue methods that are ecologically sound!

Saving on the land for the Son

Columba left his beloved Ireland for Iona with tears. Cedd left the Northumbrian hills for the flatlands of Essex, and clearly missed his native geography, for he kept returning. Aidan had to use the king as interpreter when he arrived in Northumbria as it was a strange culture. They made tough decisions about where to live for the sake of the gospel, giving up native comforts, safety, and the known.

Jesus gave up the glory of heaven for the harshness of earth, and came 'down the social ladder'. All this is in stark contrast to the pressure we face to choose where we live on the basis of nice surroundings, quiet neighbourhood, good schools and so on. Christian incarnational living on the land involves being prepared, like the Celtic saints, to move to difficult areas, where there may be few or no Christians, in order to share the message of God's love. Moving from the leafy country to the inner-city may be more in keeping with the gospel than the usual Christian flight from city estates to the suburban Bible-belt!

Praying for the land with the Spirit

Different places have different 'atmospheres'. One neighbourhood may feed hot gossip, another violence, loneliness or depression. Others exude peace, friendship or excitement. Churches do the same. Some may encourage prayer, growth and joy, others have a history of conflict, unanswered prayer, and division. As homes may need exorcising, so may some churches. As the land may be blessed and be fruitful – physically or spiritually – so may buildings. The very stones seem to be able to absorb the activity of humans. Cuthbert, Cedd and Fursey all exorcised their sites, to great effect as history shows. A circle of crosses was often erected around monasteries symbolizing that within the circle the ground was hallowed, and evil was not to enter. The land was claimed as a place where 'heaven and earth met'. There is surely every reason for Christians today to pray for that whether at home, at work, in church, in the shopping mall, in a hotel, at a garage or wherever . . .!

Group reflections

1. If you were to form a local environmental action group, what would be its priorities? How could you make it clear this action arose directly from your Christian understanding of God's world?

2. Read Philippians 2.6-8. Why do we find it easy to allow 'missionaries' to live and work in deprived areas, but often find it hard to do so ourselves? What are the consequences for those left behind if Christians, like everyone else, simply move *up* to 'nicer' neighbourhoods?

3.	Have you ever felt uneasy in a particular place? Have you any experience of exorcising a person or place? How would you go about this if asked?

4.	What difference would it make to the atmosphere of your neighbourhood if your church ceased to exist?

within myself

Today, many search for spiritual awareness but do not find it in our churches, and so go off down New Age roads or into cults or the occult. Millions attend church each week yet fail to meet the one person they hope for – God. Churches can be full of furniture, activity, words or music, yet empty of God. The reason is simple: if during the week we never pray, open our Bibles, or consider God, and expect Sunday to give us the necessary spiritual 'top up', we will be disappointed. Corporate worship works like a bucket: it is only as the congregation bring into Sunday their experience and awareness of God during the week, and 'pour' it into the corporate activity, that the spiritual level of the church rises like water in a bucket. The more who do that, the easier it is for everyone to dive in and bathe in that awareness of God. In the Celtic churches there was a recognition that ultimately we find God within our own souls, not in places, even church buildings. The need is for Christians to work with that *'inner prayer cell'* we all carry around within us.

The disciple John is credited with taking the gospel to Egypt. He who sat next to Jesus at the Last Supper and later wrote epistles about Christian love, was given the symbol of the eagle, the bird who represents how the soul can soar to heaven. It was in Egypt that the Desert Fathers and Mothers developed the first monasteries, turning their backs on the compromized church as it became increasingly official, accepted and respectable. They went out to pray and to develop the soul.

Ninian in Scotland adapted that model with his settlement at Whithorn, and it is not surprizing that John became the apostolic guru for the Celts who carved eagles onto their crosses, along with pictures of Desert Fathers like Anthony of Egypt and Paul of Thebes. Ninian developed a prayer cell in his cave at Whithorn, Cuthbert had his island in the Farnes, Herbert had his island in Derwentwater, Guthlac had his hermitage in the Fens, Baldred went to Bass Rock near Berwick, and some Irish monks went to Skellig Michael.

These monks did not go off to find God, but to develop their relationship with him. Their little bee-hive huts were prayer cells within which they entered into the cells of their hearts. They understood the promise of Jesus, 'Behold, I stand at the door and knock. If anyone hears my voice and opens the door I will come in . . .' (Revelation 3).

There is a story from the Desert Fathers: a monk decided he was fed up with his fellow monks and so decided to flee to the desert. As he was putting on his sandals he saw another monk in his cell, who he had never seen before, also putting on sandals. 'Who are you?' he said. The strange monk replied, 'I am your temptation: wherever you go, I will go first.' The moral is clear: to go off alone, or deeper within ourselves, can never be escapism: it is about confronting the reality we often avoid in company.

These were people who listened to God in stereo, with both the mind and the heart. Today we give pre-eminence to the mind, analyzing everything, and consequently we often fail to develop the Celtic art of imagination and seeing visions (as did Patrick, Fursey and Ninian).

When we read the lives of these saints, it becomes clear that often the record follows a pattern which we can use for our own spiritual development.

Group reflections

1. Saints' stories usually begin with tales about their **birth and infancy**, and how people saw something of the hand of God on them even then. What are your earliest memories? With hindsight, can you reflect on some important memory that carries a spiritual truth?

2. Saints all had a **soul-friend**. With whom do you share your deepest feelings and your spiritual journey?

3. They have recorded something about the **spiritual lead** they gave others. Who has looked to you for such a lead – family, friends, adults, children? You kid yourself if you think there is no one!

4. Their biographers wrote about how they **laid their faith on the line**. What have you done, where have you been, what have you said, and who have you met, specifically because you are a Christian?

5. Examples are given of how these people **listened to God with their hearts** and not just the mind. When have you heard that little inner voice, felt words come into your mind or had some picture that refuses to go away – some dream, hunch, feeling, prayer, concern?

6. Finally, it is always recorded **how they died** – usually ready and willing to enter the glory of heaven. While we cannot record that for ourselves (!) we can prepare ourselves for that great journey.

As we write down these things about ourselves so we record our own spiritual journey. Few of us are spiritual giants, just ordinary people. But God is precisely the God of the ordinary. It is as these Celtic saints grasped God in the ordinary, understood that God is all around ready to be spotted, that they grew into the giants they were. It is about opening the door of the soul, realizing that God is deep within, recognizing that we are 'like fish in the sea searching for the ocean' (De Mello). There is no 'fast food industry' when it comes to spiritual growth: that takes time. You may have enjoyed those '3D' pictures – images in which, if we stare long enough at the page, gradually an elephant emerges charging across the plains! To focus takes time, whether it is with the physical or with the inner eye.

The Celtic churches grew dramatically because a handful put effort into developing their inner souls. As they met, so the 'bucket' of church life filled so others could dive in and enjoy God. The same opportunity today lies within our churches – not the stones of the walls but rather the 'living stones' of the human church.

Now, can you write a simple account of your life in the style of a Celtic saint's life?

for the local church

AD 664 was a watershed year, for that is when the crucial Synod of Whitby was held. Those with a Celtic background met those with a Continental approach, in order to resolve how church life should be organized in these islands. It was a clash of personalities and emphases which, typical of church debates, dominated the issues.

Today, churches easily group themselves into those which are concerned with the 'soundness' of preachers' doctrines, or which meet as an aesthetic culture-club. Others feed on every new chorus composed, others are bent on hectic social activity, while others can seem like a social club for those who like singing hymns! Then there are those who are fed up with the whole spectrum and are always ready to leave and start a new church! So what streams are evident within the Celtic churches?

Catholic

There was a deep understanding of what it meant to belong to the universal church. They were not organized in a hierarchical organization, but rather belonged to a loose network. There was no uniform liturgy, hymn book, episcopal authority, central strategy, or central funding. While David in Wales was very strict and ascetic in the leadership of his monastery, at Coldingham in Northumbria the laxness was alarming. On Iona, Columba allowed no women, while at Whitby Hilda ruled over a monastery of both men and women. When a missioner was needed in one place, help was simply requested from another community. They were very varied in practice, united by no organization, but powerfully held together by their relationship to God rather than to an institution. That is the *true* nature of a catholic church.

Evangelical

Bishops and clergy were only appointed *after* they proved themselves as effective evangelists. Aidan, Cuthbert, and Cedd all understood how to be missionaries from within the local culture, hence the monks shaved their heads in the same style as the Druidic holy men. The Celtic crosses were simply developments of the Druid standing stones. Existing holy wells and graves were adopted and now Christian stories were told around them. As a result of this enfolding, rather than confronting, approach, the Christian faith spread like wildfire. It was conextualized mission. The implication for today is that churches need to discover, not how to import an evangelistic tool or method, but how to relate within the immediate local context – local dialect, jargon, stories, places, and events, are the starting points.

Charismatic

The Gifts of the Spirit (1 Corinthians 12) were commonly in evidence. There are literally thousands of stories of the Celtic saints praying successfully for healing. Some quite bizarre: for example, Cieren healed folk by baking bread for them! Similarly, stories of prophecy abound, for example, David's father observed a stag, a fish and some bees. He understood that his as yet unborn son would be powerful (like a stag), drink only water (like a fish), and have wisdom hidden in his character (as bees hide honey in the comb). Herbert on Derwentwater, Cuthbert on the Farnes, and Guthlac on the Fens all discerned spirits. There was an understanding that these spiritual gifts were given not simply for personal enjoyment, but as tools to further the kingdom of God. It is worth adding they also prayed for and received the New Testament gifts of celibacy and poverty, which tend to figure less prominently in our comfortable (therefore less effective?) church today!

Seasonal

Today's church calendar is derived from a Mediterranean climate: Lent and abstinence in February is sensible in southern Italy, but if taken seriously in Scotland may lead potentially to death! Baptism by immersion in rivers is sensible in Mediterranean Israel, but less so in Wales. The Celtic churches adopted the Druidic seasonal rhythm of the context, and for example, Samheim in November was when the Druids related closely to the 'other world' of spirits and the departed. This was subsumed into All Souls' Day and All Saints' Day. The winter was seen as the time to retire for prayer and study, while the summer was the time to go out sharing the faith. Church calendars and programmes 'went with the flow'. All churches can ponder how far that is happening in their programmes today.

Personal

The focus was never on buildings. Churches were usually constructed of wood, and rarely expensively decorated. If a church became too small for their needs or fell into disrepair, then another would be built. They would never be in the position of inheriting a local church building which for historical reasons was now in an inappropriate place, was the wrong size, or inordinately expensive to maintain! Today so many resources meant for mission are sucked into maintaining buildings that the real purpose of the Christian Church – to share the love of Christ with *people* – is forgotten. Their money was used to buy slaves their freedom and to feed the poor. Then, as now, the use of finances demonstrates true priorities. Church accounts are not just a legal record, they are a record of actual priorities, and when seen like that make sober reading!

Renewal

These were churches open to God, open to change, loose to organization, yet powerfully close to God. Catholic, evangelical, charismatic, seasonal and personal were not sub-groupings dividing various emphases. They were understandings taken on board by all the churches.

Group reflections

1. What, in reality, links your church to other local churches: belief, practice, style, or is it something much deeper? How strong are those ties? Can they be developed?

2. Read Ephesians 4.1-16. How might your church develop local people's ministries, especially that of evangelism?

3. Examine your church's calendar of events. How far is it governed by the church's year, the school year, or the natural year? Could things be organized more helpfully?

4. Examine your church accounts from last year. What does this show about your priorities? Should anything be changed? (Is change an acceptable word?)

with life and death

Our present generation is obsessed with origins – how the cosmos began, how the human species evolved, and how our family tree developed. Origins fascinate, but destinies seem to petrify. Life is a journey from the womb to the tomb – that is inevitable. Yet popular hope for medical advance focuses on extending life rather than enhancing its quality, and funeral services now offer 'managed' events with taped music, formica altars, and silently gliding curtains, all designed to make it feel as if nothing dramatic has happened. Bereavement seems so hard to face, and yet always gives rise to shock, numbness, despair, tears, rage, depression, inactivity or hyperactivity. The behaviour patterns are common across all social and age groups.

In 1989 the FA Cup semi-final saw Liverpool play Nottingham Forest at Hillsborough. Crowd-control failed and millions watched on television as 94 people died on the terraces. The reaction in Liverpool broke all the usual rules about death:

- the rule was broken that death is a taboo subject: spontaneous public grief broke through the normal British reserve;

- the edges became blurred: formal and informal, sacred and secular. The following day at Mass in the Roman Catholic Cathedral a huge Liverpool Football Club banner was hung and the cathedral choir sang an anthem which combined the club's song 'You'll never walk alone' with Psalm 23, 'Even though I walk through the valley of the shadow of death, I will fear no evil, for thou art with me.'

English reserve gave way to Celtic expressiveness. In Liverpool the background of many (especially of the Catholics) is Irish, Scottish and Welsh – Celtic. That heritage left them not power*less*, but with a power*ful* legacy on which to draw.

The legacy of blessing

When Columba arrived on Iona he prayed for 30 years to do his work. During those three decades he achieved enormous feats. As he realized his time was up, he prayed for an extension of four years, not through fear, but because there was still work to do. At the end of those four years, he was taken by cart around the island to bless the land, people and animals. He then gave a prophecy that before the end of the world, after a time of desolation, the island would again become a base for mission. This century his prophecy has come true with the dawn of the Iona Community. Iona has ever since been associated with Columba. We too can reflect on what blessing we leave on the places and people we have known.

The legacy of prayer

As Cuthbert lay dying, he chose a particular monk to serve his meals – a monk suffering from diarrhoea(!). As he entered Cuthbert's cell, so the holy man prayed and healed the monk. He was physically weak, but spiritually very alive. The moral is clear: even as our own bodies begin to slow down there is no reason why our prayers cannot be effective for others.

138

The legacy of togetherness

A monk in Northumbria called Drythelm was in the grip of the plague. His family gathered around and in the middle of the night he seemed to pass away. Only his wife stayed with him. Suddenly Drythelm sat up saying, 'Do not be afraid! I have risen from the grasp of death and am allowed to live amongst people again.' He recounted his 'near death experience' of being led by an angel to see something both of hell and of heaven. His testimony was powerful, and when he became a monk at Melrose his tales converted many.

His story reminds us that the distance between heaven and earth is very thin indeed. Those who are our believing friends and family are very near us. This is not spiritualism, but an affirmation of the credal statement, 'I believe in the communion of saints' – 'I believe that those in heaven are as near to me as those neighbours in the next seat!' It is only the dullness of our perception that makes heaven seem so far away.

The legacy of release

Caedmon was a monk under the authority of Hilda in the monastery at Whitby. As he received communion for the last time he asked the other monks and nuns to gather round him. He said, 'If any of you are angry with me, or if any of you hold anything against me, then I forgive you. Will you now please forgive me if I have angered you?' His time of dying became an occasion of forgiveness and release.

All these examples concern managing our farewells. It is good to be with relatives and friends at times of bereavement and for each to spend time alone with the deceased saying 'goodbye, thank you, and sorry'. It is about making peace with the person on their final journey. Then all can gather together without any sense of pretence, and commend the person to God.

A family was squabbling about how much their uncle had left. As the solicitor opened the will they shouted, 'Tell us, how much did he leave?' The solicitor said just two words: 'Absolutely everything!' We put enormous energy into sorting out our material legacy. Yet what is far more important is our spiritual legacy – and that will be determined wholly by the spiritual treasures we have accumulated during our lifetime.

Group reflections

1. 'I *am*' not 'I do' is the name by which God is known (Exodus 3.14). Made in his image we are 'human *beings*' not 'human doings!' We are more likely to be remembered for who we are than what we did. How would you like to be remembered?

2. Read 2 Kings 2. The 'mantle' of Elijah fell on Elisha. What specific Christian work of yours could be continued by someone else?

3. What sort of Christian ministry or presence would you appreciate when your time comes to enter heaven?

4. In a 100 years' time, what legacy will your church have left behind?

living on the edge

When Columbanus reached Rome, the Pope asked him to state where he was from. He replied, 'We are inhabitants of the world's edge.' Many Celtic monasteries were deliberately sited on the edge of the land: Iona, Lindisfarne, Whitby, Whithorn, Bradwell, Skellig Michael and so on. The edge is always exciting. Walking on a cliff top we need to keep alert or we fall. We see horizons others do not. Body and soul face each other. There is no escape from the self. Projections cannot be put onto others. We have to rely on our own inner resources.

In the Bible, the edge is, paradoxically, central. Jacob saw his vision of the heavenly ladder in the middle of nowhere. It was similar for Moses and his vision of the burning bush. John the Baptist burst in from the wilderness, as did Jesus. In the desert, away from the centre of human life, God fills each moment. Escapism is not in being alone, for solitude and quiet is where reality is engaged with. Escapists today are the holidaymakers, the television addicts and the workaholics.

Jesus lived always on the edge. He was born in a manger, of unmarried parents, an infant refugee, homeless. He touched lepers, ate with prostitutes, then was edged out of the synagogue, the temple, the city, and even life itself. Yet he was more in touch with reality than those in the palace, the fortress or the government office. Similarly, the church has always been renewed by those pushed to the edge: St Francis and John Wesley are two obvious historical examples.

Today, increasingly, we become 'midlanders', all identical in clothing, bound by bureaucracy, and herded into shopping malls. The Celtic Christians went rather to new boundaries. They prayed for hours in the North Sea, arms outstretched cruciform style. They were combative and contemplative in prayer. They saw visions and had vision. They knew the Gospels by heart. Their imagery in their art was eccentric and celebratory – not the product of an official committee! They met God in their cells: the individual beehive huts in which they sat, where they travelled even further into the inner cells of their hearts. They walked the cliff top of isolation. They would 'waste time' with God on pilgrimage, letting God carry them with the waves and currents of life. They had no obsession with strategies, but rather travelled light, resolving always to move on both physically and spiritually. They were not controlled by the dictates of a central management or office, but realized it was the credibility of their personal journey with God – both in their human and in their inner life – that gave credibility to their words. Their sheer holiness and close walk with God attracted others to join them at their inaccessible sites.

The focus for their church life was not the vicar, the church building, the church council, the Sunday service, or the calendar of events. Rather, the focus was the whole community. They understood that because God is community and we are built in his image, then we find our fulfilment when we are in community. They shared their meals, work and prayers. Not for them the individualism that increasingly dominates our society, and which paradoxically, our whole society seems to worship.

The Celtic churches relied on no false props of money or possessions. Pope Gregory told Augustine that of all money given, one quarter was to go to the bishops, one quarter to the clergy, one quarter to hospitality, and one quarter to the poor: the Celtic churches simply gave away all to the poor. They were deliberately vulnerable.

The Celtic churches were not organized centrally or hierarchically, but rather acted as a loose federation, each trusting the other to do what was right in each place. Each was free to go its own way, diverse in practice yet orthodox in belief. Today, what is right for the inner city, the new town, the rural, the suburb and the city centre will each be different. The way each church devises its own liturgy, evangelizes, cares pastorally, teaches children, manages its business, will vary. Each needs to ask, 'what for us here is the equivalent issue of the Druid haircut for our holy leaders, the Celtic darkened room for school children, the high crosses developed from standing stones, the sacred wells and graves needing to be absorbed and re-used'? For each place, the answer will be different. It is about having confidence to be ourselves in our own place. It is about finding God in the present place and people and culture. It is about ridding ourselves of the organizational clutter that so easily takes us from our two main priorities: prayer and mission. That was the secret of the Celtic churches.

It is true today that many find new life in the prayers of David Adam, in the liturgies of Iona, and in the pilgrimages to Celtic sites. Shops contain shelves full of books on Celtic material. Celtic workshops are overbooked. But the danger is that anything which becomes respectable risks being brought from the edge to the centre. Once we move inland from the cliff edge the element of risk evaporates and the adrenalin ceases to pump so quickly. We rely less on God's resources and more on institutional props. Is that not why Cuthbert at first refused to be brought from his Farne Island to be made a bishop?

A church wishing to be true to the Celtic tradition will not simply say, 'If we copy this, that and the other, then we will be Celtic in nature.' But rather it will continually ask, 'How do we keep ourselves on the spiritual edge?' For the edge is always the centre of spiritual renewal.

Group reflections

1. Moses, John the Baptist and Jesus all had profound spiritual experiences in the solitude of the desert. Why is solitude today often perceived as escapism rather than engaging with reality? Do you have any experiences to share?

2. Where do you experience imagining exciting new Christian possibilities?

3. Which Christians in the twentieth century have been 'on the edge' and yet vitally central in their effect globally? What new horizons or possibilities did they see?

4. Read Revelation 7.9-12. John had a vision of worship in heaven. What is your dream for your church? Is it of God? What risks are involved? Could it bring renewal for your church and others? How can you work towards it? Will you go for it?

artistic activities

introduction

The activities suggested here are not meant to be an exhaustive list, but rather an indication of some of the fun to be had while musing on some of the insights of Celtic spirituality. They have all been tested and tried with different groups, many with both children and adults. The settings have ranged from an open-air festival to a professional In-Service Training session for teachers to a project attempted by a small group.

What is crucial is to remember that the Celtic monks produced their work as an act of worship and as an aid to worship and meditation. That does not mean it was all extremely serious and tense, but simply that there was a reason behind it all. Consequently, as many of the activities employ Celtic knotwork as a basis, the contents of the next section, *Understanding Celtic knotwork*, should be conveyed to those taking part. For all participants, the crucial question is not, 'Did I produce a magnificent work of art?', for the end result is less important than the process. A true assessment will ask, 'Has this helped my understanding of God and so encouraged my spiritual development?'

understanding celtic knotwork

Knotwork designs are seen everywhere on tee-shirts, jewellery, mugs, coasters and book-marks, yet most of those who buy these designs do not realize what great spiritual visual aids they are! These interlocking designs are highly stylized and complex: they are no mere 'taking a pencil for a walk'!

From the fifth to the ninth century each monastery would have copies of the Gospels and the Psalms, each decorated in the style we see so amazingly preserved in examples such as the Book of Kells and the Lindisfarne Gospels. The vast majority, of course, have not survived due to both Viking raids on coastal monasteries, and the ravages of time since most decoration was on wood or parchment. Stone crosses, church doorways and jewellery remain as our major source of clues.

The designs were never intended just to be pretty patterns, but to communicate deep truths about God and about life. Therein lies our problem: when *words* are used to explain what is understood to be *beyond words*, then the power of the designs is diminished. But what are we meant to grasp?

1. God is one

Just as the traced patterns have no end, neither has God. The Celts believed that the devil is frustrated by anything that has no break in it, no doorway for access. Hence the unbroken line and the circle were important. Monasteries were often circular, the encircling *caim* prayers were said for protection, and coffins in the Hebrides are still sometimes carried around the graveyard symbolically to pray for the protection of the dead.

2. God is community

In some of the simplest designs God is seen to be eternally one yet Trinity. God is a love affair between the three, each mutually supporting, sending and receiving the others. As a traditional Celtic poem says:

> Three folds of the cloth, yet only one napkin is there,
> Three joints of the finger, yet only one finger fair,
> Three leaves of the shamrock, yet only one shamrock to wear,
> Frost, snowflake and ice, all in water their origin share,
> Three persons in God, yet to one God alone we make prayer.

To draw the threefold picture of God explains the Trinity in a way that words can never do.

3. Life is one

Many designs involve twisting sinuous animals, flowers, people and plants. They demonstrate a primitive awareness that everything shares its origin in God and is part of one interwoven life, one great eco-system. There is no division between God and his creation. It is not that creation is God, nor is it pantheism. It is about creation being a sacrament, an image of God in which the very nature of God, his oneness, is demonstrated.

4. Communal society

Many designs have stylized human figures which interlock and flow from each other. Here there is the suggestion that just as God is one, so humanity made in his image is also to be ordered as a united society. Individualism and loneliness can never be a true reflection of God. The Celts were highly tribal and the extended family was central. Christian expression of this was natural in the establishing of monasteries as extended families.

5. Pilgrimage

The Celts were wanderers by nature. They loved their homes but they loved to explore, for exploring creation is to explore God's handiwork and so discover more of the nature of God the creator. The knotwork is no mere meandering trail. It has a definite pattern that can often only be seen when one stands back from it. That is a picture of our lives. It is often easy for us to feel that our lives are pointless and aimless, but it is as we stand back we begin to discern a pattern in the hands of the master-craftsman. Jesus is the 'way', the 'alpha and the omega': we travel with him as 'people of the way', often twisting to and fro in life, covering the same ground time and again, yet always different because of the intervening experiences.

6. Mystery

Words which explain such patterns are nonsense! As our lives twist to and fro, so our days are a mystery. We do not know what will affect us tomorrow. There will be new ideas, experiences, relationships; new depths of love, new insights to explore. Maybe as our outer eye ponders the patterns on the page so our inner eye can ponder the nature of God, the state of our souls, and our relationship with God and his creation.

That is a process which can never cease, just as the lines of the patterns never cease. These are not just pretty shapes to see and then pass on. The pilgrim is invited to stop and ponder, whether through looking at a twentieth-century tee-shirt or a seventh-century stone cross. As we do that so we allow God to take us on a journey which will make a difference to us, and so to the people we meet and the world in which we are set.

Designing a
Celtic pattern

Most people communicate most readily with words, but symbols and patterns can not only portray real truth, but do so in a way which both demands and allows the viewer to meditate and to consider for himself.

As an exercise for individuals, choose:

> one **person** who is or has been important in your life;
>
> one **place** which has been or is significant to you;
>
> one **event** which has shaped your life;
>
> one **truth about God** which excites you at your present stage in life.

For the sake of this exercise, it does not actually matter what your choices are – it is the exercise not the content that is important.

Now draw a caricature of each of these four as the Celtic artists did – cartoon-style not definitive classical art!

Each of these four may appear unrelated, but do in fact meet in you! They connect and intertwine in your memory and in your soul. So now create a knotwork pattern showing how these four connect in you (see pages 149-50 for instructions on creating knotwork patterns). Use no words but demonstrate this in such a way that those who look at your created pattern may begin to surmise something about your life.

A similar exercise can be done to sum up something as apparently literary as a **curriculum vitae**! Choose several qualifications, jobs, responsibilities, interests and aspirations, and then create a knotwork pattern to show how your life has proceeded, twisted to and fro, and how it might proceed.

This can also be done to demonstrate the unity of your **hobbies** or interests, the relationships with your **family**, your circle of **friends**, or your **Christian journey**.

In creating such patterns take time. Do not worry about the end result. It is the doing of it that is the challenge to the soul, not the completed design. As always, the destination is, in fact, the journey itself!

a guíðe to creating celtíc knotwork

for the adventurous

1. Place a sheet of plain paper on template of diagonal squares. Line it up like this:

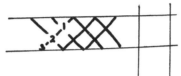

2. For a three-way plait, draw a line along a row of diagonal intersections.

   Count three diagonal squares, and draw a second line in pencil.

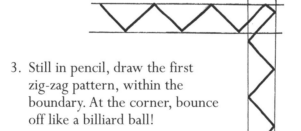

3. Still in pencil, draw the first zig-zag pattern, within the boundary. At the corner, bounce off like a billiard ball!

4 a. From the same point, add zig zag ②

   b. and zig-zag ③

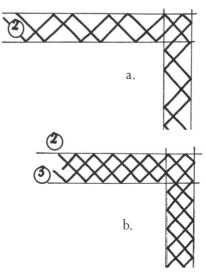

a.

b.

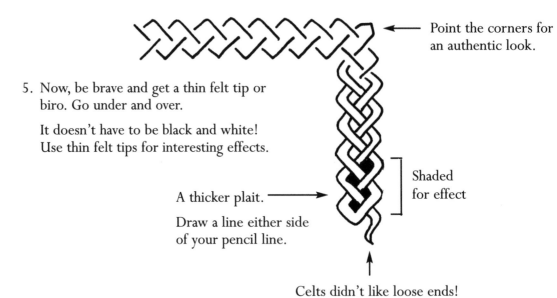

Point the corners for an authentic look.

5. Now, be brave and get a thin felt tip or biro. Go under and over.

   It doesn't have to be black and white! Use thin felt tips for interesting effects.

A thicker plait. ———————>

Draw a line either side of your pencil line.

Shaded for effect

Celts didn't like loose ends! Use your imagination. Is it a cat's tail, a dragon's head, or what?

6. Taking it further.

   Now try a four plait!

Don't forget to rub your guidelines out!

Of course, plaits don't have to be linear — they can double back and loop . . .

Go loopy . . .

1. Here are guidelines for a four plait.
   Mark in pencil intersecting points every four spaces.
   (I have chosen every other one along the bottom row.)

2. Whenever you meet a line, double back.
   This is the only rule.

3. Now, experiment!
   Try marking lines five spaces apart.
   A three-plait pattern is evolving
   – good for trinitarian prayers!

A note on corners . . .

Fig. 1

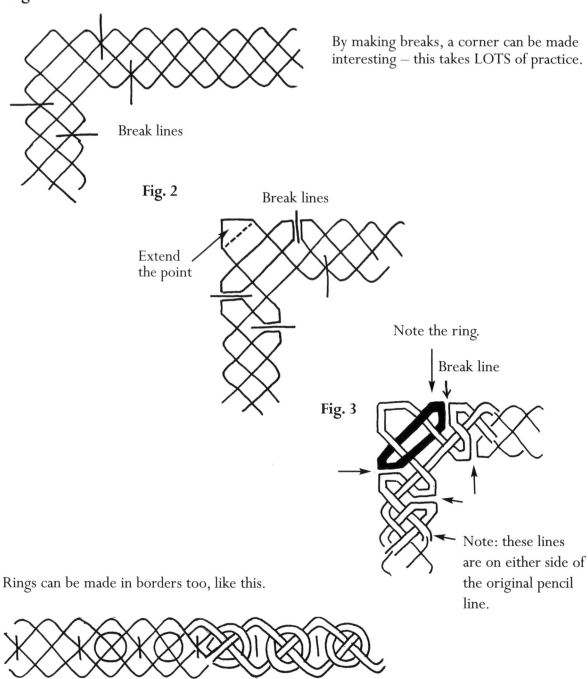

By making breaks, a corner can be made interesting – this takes LOTS of practice.

Break lines

Fig. 2

Break lines

Extend the point

Note the ring.

Break line

Fig. 3

Note: these lines are on either side of the original pencil line.

Rings can be made in borders too, like this.

Rings can intersect . . . which gets complicated but fun.

© Fran Wakefield

all-age activities

Once a choice has been made about people or places or themes to incorporate (as outlined in the section above, Designing a Celtic pattern, p.148) then any of the following can be tried:

1. Simply **draw** the design using crayons, paint, felt-pens etc. Often it helps to use squared grid paper as it is easier then to make patterns symmetrical. Think about what you are trying to express through the pattern, rather than just 'take your pencil for a walk' to see what emerges. The ancient scribes and artists were painstaking in their effort and were clear they were doing it for the glory of God and the edification of others. But don't be afraid to use humour if, for example, you want to portray a person or an event in cartoon form. Perhaps you might create a **birthday card** for someone with a design that pulls together aspects of their life. Pam Pott (Fountaingate Community, 58 Geoffrey Road, London SE4 1NT) produces some delightfully original **Christmas cards** as well as material for other occasions. Tim Tiley Prints (Eblana Lodge, 157 Cheltenham Road, Bristol BS6 5RR) and Lindsey Attwood (40 Walter Street, Derby DE1 3PR) also produce a large variety of cards and designs and may help to stimulate your ideas.

2. **Plasticine or clay** can be used to create a more 3D effect. It will probably be best to plan on paper first and to keep your designs very simple especially at first. Simple lace-knotwork can be made using thin rolls of your material, while any symbols you incorporate are best cut from flat sheets and attached to the lacing. What about using **icing on a birthday cake** and decorating the flat top to indicate some of the person's hobbies or interests? Can you create a suitable design for a **Christmas cake**?

3. Western Christians often tend to be very word-centred, whereas some other world religions are more open to symbolism. Asian Muslim and Hindu women and girls will decorate their hands with patterns, called mendhi, using henna paste either drawn on or painted over stencils. Similarly, Celtic designs can be drawn on one's own body, or, for fun, on each other's! Celtic warriors, after all, were well-known for their body painting! In western culture children especially enjoy **face paints** which can be used on hands, arms, faces and chests. Do plan the design on paper first in order not to let it descend into a messy time of total chaos.

4. **Bookmarks** can be made using card. Cut out pieces of blank card about 15 x 5cm.

    - If people are encouraged to create their own patterns, it often helps to design first on paper and then trace through onto the card, since card can be expensive.

    - Alternatively, cards can be provided with designs already photocopied onto them. People are then invited to add one or two caricatures onto the ends of designs and colour the whole pattern.

- There are many books available showing the alphabet written in Celtic styles, and these can be used to give a monogram of the initial of the person's name at the centre of the design.

- A method younger children often enjoy involves buying ink stamps of Celtic designs which are now available in many craft shops, and simply colouring them.

5. On a day when workshops are planned and a simple meal or picnic is part of the programme **plastic spoons** can be decorated with Celtic patterns using indelible felt-pens or pens designed for use with overhead projector acetates. Obviously the patterns need to be very basic because the space is so limited. **Paper plates** can also be decorated with indelible felt pens.

6. **Flags** can be made using 10 x 10cm squares of paper, card or old sheets stuck onto bamboo canes or small plant canes. Children especially enjoy these outdoors. A good group exercise is to create a large flag or banner together. Fabric paints or crayons are best if large areas are to be coloured. The simple process of working together on a piece of art can be an exercise in exploring the dynamics of community in itself, and so give material for group reflection later.

7. **Badge-making machines** can often be hired locally from play associations. Designs are photocopied or drawn onto circular pieces of paper and then coloured with crayons or felt pens. The paper is then sealed under a clear acetate cover and clamped onto a blank tin badge.

Designing knotwork patterns need not be the preserve of adults. Children too will begin to understand something of the significance of them as they create their own and are often very intuitive with symbolic design.

Any of these ideas can be used at workshops, awaydays, retreats, parties, fêtes, holiday club activities, or Sunday School events. Invariably, it is as the activities are explained that the notions behind the concept of Celtic knotwork are revealed.

sewing cross-stitch patterns

1 — Creating your own

Materials

Probably the best fabric for a beginner is Aida. This has a woven grid which creates blocks, and each stitch is made over one block. Aida comes in different sizes depending on how many holes per inch (hpi) there are. The easiest to start with is size 14: 14 hpi.

The thread or floss is bought in skeins which is divided into strands depending on what the pattern suggests. Tapestry needles are used for cross-stitch, and for size 14 Aida then size 22 or 24 needles would be best.

Getting started

Start sewing by bringing the needle through the fabric from behind, leaving a short length of thread at the back of the cloth. This excess should be secured by later stitches as you move along. Make your first cross as in Figure 1. Most patterns have rows or blocks of stitches where you can move first in one direction and then return to complete the crosses as in Figure 2.

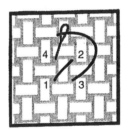

Fig. 1

The pattern below (Fig. 3) shows two symbols which relate to two colours: leave any blank squares. When you have finished the design it may need to be pressed – place the fabric face down on a towel and use a cool or medium iron.

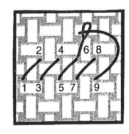

Fig. 2

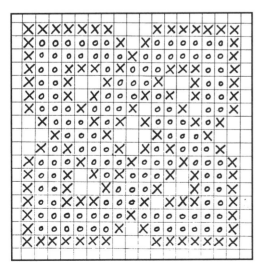

Fig. 3

© Hazel Palmer

155

sewing cross-stitch patterns

2 – following a pre-set design

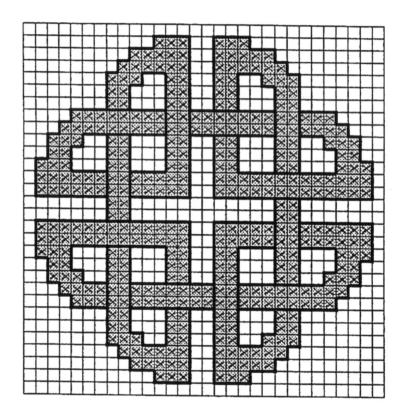

Preparation

1. Edges of fabric can be neatened by hemming or zigzagging to prevent fraying.

2. It is very important to centralize the design, so fold the fabric in half horizontally and vertically and, by tacking, mark the centre lines.

Following the chart above

One square on the chart – one stitch.

Cross stitch

1. Use pre-cut lengths of thread each time to avoid knotting and tangling. Strip the thread by taking off one strand at a time. Lay two strands together for stitching. By doing this, you will create a smoother stitch.

2. Never start or finish with a knot. It is better to thread the needle through stitches already worked. Do not carry long threads from one area to another. It is better to finish and start afresh.

3. Ensure that the diagonal of each cross-stitch is worked in the same direction. Try to make the back as neat as possible.

4. When you have finished the whole design, outline with backstitching using one strand of black thread.

© Val Butler

Simple and inexpensive kits containing all the materials, with instructions, a card for mounting, and an explanation of the symbolism of knotwork are available from: Aquila Celtic Crafts, White Lyons Cottage, High Street, Bradwell-on-Sea, Essex CMO 7HN, Tel: 01621 776438.

celtic jewellery methods

All these methods will use the same design as it is a simple shape to start with. More intricate designs could be attempted with more practice. Most equipment and materials used can be obtained from a DIY shop or a craft shop. A good craft shop will also be able to help with suppliers for items such as metal and soldering equipment. Because of the processes involved this is obviously not an activity suitable for children, and adults will need supervising at first. At all times, personal safety is paramount.

Pierced jewellery

Draw your design onto a sheet of metal (approx. 1mm thick) and cut out with a piercing saw. To remove the negative shapes in the middle, first drill a small hole, insert the piercing saw blade, tighten saw and cut out. Piercing will be a lot easier if you use a vice to hold your metal. To add detail where the lines cross each other, either score these with a scribe or other sharp tool, or use a punching tool and hammer to make a shallow indentation. Smooth off any rough edges with a needle file or  some wet and dry paper. A small wire ring could be attached to the top of your piece, or incorporated into your pierced pattern to attach it to a chain etc. The pierced method would work well for a Celtic cross design.

Cast jewellery

Make a master piece out of everyday materials such as some string glued onto a piece of card.

 Make sure there are not undercuts as this will make casting problematic.

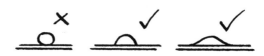

The original makers of cast Celtic jewellery would push their master piece into a slab of clay to create an impression of the design, into which they would cast their metal. This method is quick, but each impression can only be used a couple of times before it needs to be re-made. A more permanent mould can be made by building a box around your master piece, sticking it onto a base, putting Vaseline on it, and pouring plaster onto it.

158

When the plaster has set and is cold, the mould can be removed and the master piece taken out carefully (using a blunt cocktail stick may help). Be careful not to scratch the plaster impression.

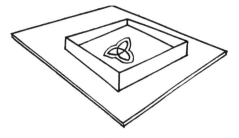

Put pieces of pewter into a metal ladle (hold handle with oven gloves), and heat with a blow torch until the pewter becomes pourable, which will not take long. Pour the molten pewter into your clay or plaster mould and leave to set. When cool, remove and file off any excess and clean up with soft wire wool.

An attachment (e.g. for a brooch) can be glued on with '2 part epoxy' or Araldite, or you could place it into the molten pewter with tweezers and allow it to set in place (pewter sets very quickly). This technique is ideal for buttons

Wire jewellery

Bend a length of wire (e.g. silver or copper) into your desired shape using flat-nosed and round-nosed pliers. Make sure the wire crosses over and under where it should. Try to keep your design as flat as possible (you may need to hammer it gently between two pieces of wood). It is important that the wire touches at the points where it crosses over.

Place your piece on a heatproof brick (make sure you find somewhere with good ventilation (e.g. by an open window, as soldering produces some fumes). Dab some silver solder flux on each join. Heat each join gently with a small soldering torch until the flux looks watery, and while holding the flame to the join, touch it with some silver solder until the solder flows into the join. Do this with each join. Any excess solder can be removed afterwards.

When all joins have been soldered, quench your piece in some cold water to harden it. You may need to flatten your piece again by hammering it gently between two pieces of wood. Clean up with soft wire wool. This method is good for items such as earrings as the piece is not heavy.

All fittings for earrings, brooches, buttons, pendants, cufflinks etc. can be purchased from a good craft shop.

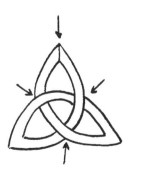

© Caroline Wallace

celtic calligraphy

This is an activity everyone can try with relatively little expense. Once mastered, it can be used to create posters for outside publicity or for internal use within church on either posters or banners. It can be used in greeting cards or notepaper. There really is no limit! However, half-uncial script is not really one for a beginner in calligraphy – but don't let that put you off! It's always fun to have a go and you may find that you're a natural and that you want to learn further. You really need an 'edged' pen, but for a taster you can try a straight-edged felt-tip pen, e.g. (Berol) italic.

Draw yourself a grid like this. The narrow space should be two widths of your pen nib, the wider space five nib widths.

| ascender |
| x-height |
| descender |
| space |

Vertical strokes are drawn with the nib horizontal, i.e. in line with the lines of your grid. Otherwise hold the pen at a 45° angle (slanted).

On curved letters, e.g. C, start at the top where the line is narrow, come round to the bottom narrow bit (stroke 1), lift off, turn nib horizontal, do stroke 2 from right to left, then stroke 3 at the top.

Hold the pen in a relaxed way and try to work with fluid movements. It will help to work on a slanted surface. Keep spaces between letters consistent. Spaces between words should be the width of a letter 'O'.

aBcoefghijklmno pQRstuvwxyz

If you want to find out more, try *Calligraphy Step-by-Step* by Gaynor Goffe or *Celtic Hand – Stroke by Stroke* by Arthur Baker.

© Pam Pott

creating a knotwork garden

This can be an exercise that is both attractive and useful in the garden, and also a source of contemplation on the meaning of Celtic knotwork for the gardener and for the visitor.

The typical plants used to form the knots themselves are box, lavender, rosemary or hyssop. Between these low hedges can be planted herbs. As the herbs die back in the autumn so the permanent outlines of the evergreen hedges clearly maintain the knotwork design. All the plants need to be low growing so that the intertwined patterns can be seen throughout the year.

First design on paper

Measure the area available exactly and draw it to scale on graph paper. Mark in the design to be planted, allowing a 9″ width for the hedging. Mark into the hedging plan the names of plants to be used, remembering that a combination of colour contrasts can give the illusion that hedges weave under and over each other, rather than simply meeting. Common box is green, cotton lavender is silvery, wall germander is deep green. Young plants should be grown 6″ apart and new growth carefully managed to create low bushy growth.

Enter the names of plants to be grown in the spaces between the hedging, having checked all the usual things – type of soil, sunny or shady, shelter etc. Be sure you know the final height of plants: herbs are the obvious choice. Balm, basil, borage, caraway, catmint, coriander, dill, fennel, feverfew, marjoram, mustard, parsley, rue, savory, sorrel, thyme, can all be tried. Decide on the number of plants, remembering many can be invasive, so do not overplant.

Now move outside

Mark the design using loose string, or better, a trail of sand trickled from a bottle. Do measure accurately: patience and care at this stage will be repaid in years to come. Write on labels the names of herbs and insert where they are to be planted, drawing a circle around them to remind yourself of the extent of their final spread.

Gravel of different colours may also be used between the hedging to accentuate the design, either in place of the herbs, or around them. Allow four years for the garden to reach maturity. Use the herbs for cooking and appreciate the garden as another source for spiritual meditation on the significance of the designs.

tattoos, stencils
and transfers

Many books of resources can be bought easily today and some are listed at the end of this book.

Tattoos are available based on ancient Celtic designs which are very cheap. These are applied to any part of the body which is free of hair. The tattoo is simply placed face down and pressed firmly, wetted with a sponge, and then the back carefully removed. (*Celtic Tattoos* by Mallory Pearce is a good example).

Stencils of all sorts are available in many shops. Some may be books of card with designs punched out so that felt pens simply colour the paper placed underneath with the design itself (e.g. *Fun with Celtic Stencils*, by Paul Kennedy). Other books contain collections of designs which need to be photocopied and then cut from card or paper (e.g. *Celtic Cut and Use Stencils* by Co Spinhoven).

Transfers also can be used. Dover Publications produce iron-on transfers of designs which can be used on cloth. In this case the designs are placed over, for example, a handkerchief or tee-shirt, and a warm iron is used. The transfers will often be effective for five or six different pieces of cloth. The designs can then be filled in or traced with fabric pens or paints.

Stained glass: Dover Publications also produce booklets of pages in which symbols from the Book of Kells and other sources are reproduced on translucent paper. The plates can be coloured and then hung or fixed onto windows or near a source of light.

There are many books with hundreds of examples of Celtic artwork which can be used to copy or to colour (see Recommended Reading p. 190). Some are copyright-free, others have simple conditions about their use, while others do not allow reproduction. *Remember:* Columba was exiled from Ireland because he copied without permission. The ruling then, as now, was that 'the calf belongs to the cow!', i.e. the copy belongs to the original!

Designing and Creating a Celtic Cross

1. Decide what truth it is that you want to portray – remember the cross is a symbolic representation, a visual aid, a story in itself. So with what sort of pictures, designs or shapes will you seek to adorn your basic cross?

2. What form of cross? Will it be a cross with four equal-length arms, or a traditional tall cross? Will it have a circle around the apex? Will the vertical beam have parallel sides or will they narrow towards the centre?

What follows is a simple step-by-step guide already used:

Step 1

I consider my own journey of life:

> When is an end an end and not a beginning?
> Or a beginning not an end?
> Before our lives were woven
> in hidden places
> the start,
> the conception,
> – we were known by you.

Full Circle by Pam Pott

Step 2

A simple equal cross for the basic shape was decided on, with a circle in the middle. The four arms were to link with an interwoven design going from birth at the bottom in a clockwise direction back round to 'birth' or rebirth in resurrection.

Step 3

Now the circle in the centre needs attention. The pilgrim is walking along a path with mountains in the background. A wild goose in the sky represents the presence of the Holy Spirit with us on the journey.

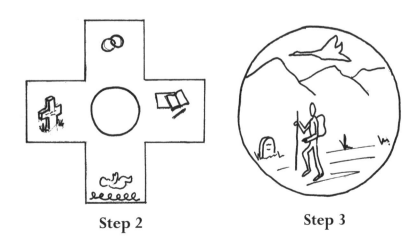

Step 2   Step 3

Step 4

The full design now needs to be worked out using an inter-woven design on squared paper.

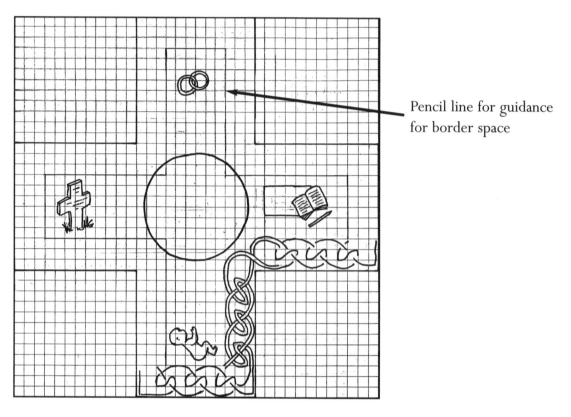

Pencil line for guidance
for border space

Step 5
The completed cross.

© Pam Pott

making a church banner

Banners in churches are increasingly becoming a regular feature. They are colourful, striking, easy to make, and can be changed easily depending on the time of year or the occasion.

First you need to decide the size required depending on where it will hang. Strong wooden dowelling might be adequate as a top bar from which to hang the banner, but if the banner is to be large and heavy then a wooden broom handle cut to size is cheap and strong. You will also need to place a similar piece of wood along the base of the banner to ensure that it hangs straight.

Hessian makes a good backing and this can be machined and hemmed leaving at both the top and the bottom an open hem large enough to insert the horizontal pole.

Cover the front of the hessian with a large single piece of background fabric, using a firm, medium-weight cloth. For the design itself, the cloth used must not be too loosely woven as it will fray too easily. The colours used should give a strong contrast between the background and the main design.

Divide the design into sections to help in drawing all the parts equal (Fig.1). Use tracings of one section to complete the design.

To make the design appear as a continuous line it has to be divided into sections and separate pattern shapes traced off (Fig.2). Each piece should be numbered to help reassemble it. Where a pattern piece end is to join a line going in another direction, an extra $1/2''$ should be added to the pattern length (Fig.3). Vilene Bondaweb (which can be bought by the metre or in a small packet) is used to secure the design to the background. Bondaweb has a smooth paper side and a rough adhesive side.

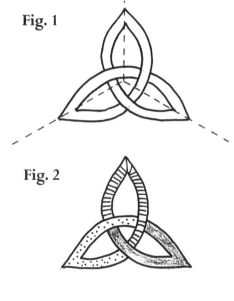

Fig. 1

Fig. 2

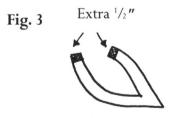

Fig. 3   Extra $1/2''$

1. Place the pattern pieces *face down* onto the paper side of the Bondaweb and draw around the shapes with a pencil. Cut them out roughly.

2. With a dry iron press the Bondaweb pattern pieces, adhesive side down, onto the *wrong side of the design fabric*.

3. The pattern pieces can then be cut out exactly along drawn lines.

4. When all the pieces are cut out peel off the paper backing, leaving the adhesive on the wrong side of the fabric.

5. Place the design pieces onto the backing fabric in their correct positions, underlapping the extra $^{1}/_{2}''$ allowed to look the same as the finished design.

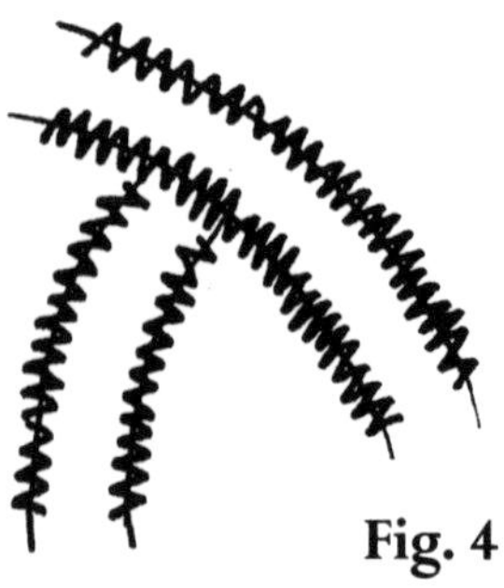

6. When all is correctly positioned, cover with a cotton cloth, and, a section at a time, press firmly using a steam iron. (The cloth can be damp if no steam iron is available.) Do not slide the iron to move over the design, but lift and put straight down on the next piece, as sliding can move the pieces out of position. The steam melts the adhesive and joins the design to the background.

Fig. 4

The banner can be left at this stage, or the design can be further secured by using a zigzag machine stitch.

Follow the way of the design, matching all the edges using a stitch length of 1–1.5 mm and a stitch width of 2–2.5 mm (fig. 4).

To prevent the background from stretching during machining, a fusible dressmaker's inter-lining can be ironed to the wrong side of the backing, behind the design.

© Glenda Abbott and Joan Houghton

making a
st Brigid's cross

In the fifth century in Ireland, Brigid tended a dying king. As she sat with him so she absent-mindedly wove a cross from the reeds on the floor. The king asked her to explain what she was doing, and as she told him the significance of the cross so he became a Christian before he died. Today such crosses are sold in Ireland, and in some places on St Brigid's Day, 1 February, her cross is hung in the house. The next year as a new one is hung in the house so the old one is hung in the barn. The following year the original cross is ploughed into the field. It is a symbolic way of praying for the house, the animals and the crops.

The cross can easily be made from reeds, rushes, iris leaves, or strips of paper

1.   Take four equal strips of paper or reed.

2.   Mark the first exactly in the centre of its length.

3.   Fold the second leaf in half around it, and to the left of its centre, leaving a gap the width of the strip.

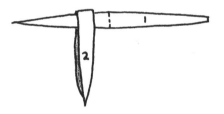

4.   Fold the third leaf in half around the second one.

5.   Fold the fourth leaf in half around the third.

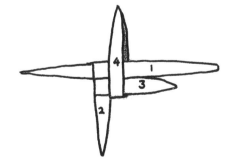

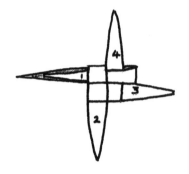

6. There are now two arms on the right. Take the single arm (1) and bend it back over 4 and through the loop of 2.

7. You now have a Brigid's cross. Tie thread around ends to hold them together, or glue.

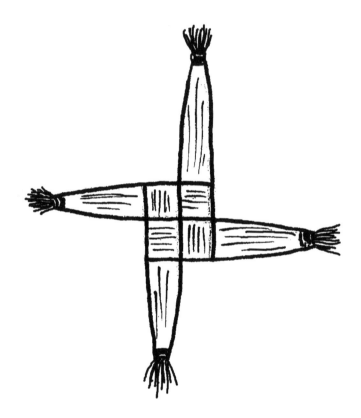

As this is being done, recall how Brigid always put her faith both into action and into words. She was a holy leader whose walk with God was so close that her prayers were effective. Her beliefs were not just ideas, but were the core of her life. Reflect on the quality of your own walk with God, and make some resolution for the future. When the cross is completed hang it in your house and ask God to bless all that happens within it – the welcoming of friends and strangers, the sharing of meals, and the comfort of companionship.

círcle-walks

Circles were significant to the Celts. It was felt that a circle with no break was a complete whole affording no access to the devil. Monasteries were often built with a circle of crosses surrounding them declaring that the space within was sacred and different – dedicated to God and claimed as a place where God met people who were offered sanctuary and hospitality. The Celtic cross with its circle at the heart of the cross drew on the significance of the sun as the source of heat and light, reminding people of the nimbus or halo that artists used to signify the white heat of pure holiness. In some Hebridean graveyards, coffins are still carried around the cemetery three times while prayers are said for the safety of the departed. Indeed, many graveyards with Saxon origins themselves are circular.

When praying for protection, the *caim* prayer would be used. The forefinger of the right hand is extended and an imaginary circle drawn around the people or place being prayed for. As the line is drawn so simple repetitive prayers are said, invoking peace or love or security in the name of the Father, and the Son and the Spirit: 'Peace be to this place in the name of the Father, etc.' Just as Cuthbert prayed to exorcise his island in the Inner Farnes, and Cedd exorcised the site for his monastery at Lastingham, so we can do the same today.

It is not uncommon today for places to acquire atmospheres that are unhelpful. Some communities or places of work can seem highly disturbed or oppressive or negative. Simply to pray can seem rather intangible. We are made as physical human beings who express ourselves physically – we kiss, shake hands, touch cloth, food and fondle carvings. It is not surprising Jesus encouraged his followers to eat bread and drink wine as an aid to remembering his sacrifice. Nor is it surprising that water is used in Christian initiation rites: drowning and rising again is rich symbolism! To express our prayers physically – and socially – can be very helpful.

In blessing a new house, each room can be entered, and a *caim* prayer used. The whole house can be circled from the outside, and so can each resident. For a community, a prayer-walk can be taken by a group stopping at significant places to pray in this way. A circle-walk can be arranged to take in a symbolic place – a house, a place of work, a school, a hospital, shops, an entertainment centre. It is simply the approach used by rural churches on Rogation Sunday or by urban churches in, for example, marches for Jesus. The walk becomes a pilgrimage, a time of prayer, an opportunity to talk and share and eat, and a chance to do what our forbears did in creating the right conditions for the advance of God's kingdom!

composing triaos

The Celtic people often became Christians fairly readily because they understood the new religion to be a fulfilment of their own pagan Druidism. They readily understood the Trinity at the heart of the Christian faith, having previously worshipped, amongst others, gods who were portrayed in three manifestations. In fact, the number three was very important to them socially. It was a mystical number. As a non-literary people they transmitted their culture, wisdom, morality, history, and religion orally. In order for this to be memorable they often created sayings in threes. It is not dissimilar to the way in which the ancient Hebrews created little sayings in the Psalms which were in twos. For example:

> Lord, you have examined me and you know me,
> You know everything I do.   (Psalm 139.1)

> It is good to sing praises to our God,
> It is pleasant and right to praise him.   (Psalm 147.1)

Similarly, the Celtic people composed in threes; for example:

> Three things that come unbidden: fear, jealousy, love.

> Three beautiful things: a full-rigged ship, a woman with child, a full moon.

> Three threads to life: the thin stream of milk from a cow, the thin blade that supports the corn, the thin thread of grace by which God holds us all.

> Three fewnesses better than plenty: a fewness of fine words, a fewness of cows in pasture, a fewness of friends around good ale.

> There are three sources of new life: a hen's egg, a woman's belly, a wrong forgiven.

> Three deaths better than life: the death of a salmon, the death of a fat pig, the death of a robber.

> Three glories of gathering: a beautiful wife, a good horse, a swift hound.

> Three things a king shares with no-one: his treasure, his hawk, his tax-man.

Three things that unlock thoughts: drunkenness, trustfulness,
love.

Three renewings of the world: a woman's womb, a cow's
udder, a smith's fire.

Three candles that illumine every darkness: truth, nature,
knowledge.

Three people with closed ears: a king bent on victory, a mer-
chant bent on profit, a monk who thinks he is holy.

There is a sense in which threes do come as naturally as ABC: 123. Perhaps there is a 'three-
someness' built into the universe by the God who is Trinity? Certainly, the Celtic Christians
were very trinitarian in their faith and in their praying.

It was an unknown Celt who wrote,

Three folds of the cloth yet only one napkin is there,
Three joints in the finger yet still only one finger fair,
Three leaves of the shamrock yet no more than one shamrock
to wear,
Frost, snowflake and ice, all in water their origin share,
Three persons in God: to one God we make our prayer.

That poem serves as a reminder of the legend that St Patrick used the shamrock to explain the
Trinity to those of his day.

To create modern triads which have a sense of flow and unity about them simply choose any
one aspect of your life, and see if you can identify three aspects which are good images or
objectives. Keep the phrases short, positive, and thematic.

A good modern example is:

Three things are pleasant in a home:
Good food upon the table;
A man who lovingly kisses his wife;
Children who refrain from quarrelling.

Three attitudes are godly in the Church:
True love of the Lord himself;
Kindness amongst the pews;
A fair dealing with self.

Three ideas enlarge a man's mind:
A humble heart;
A generous soul;
Honesty in business.

Three things I wish for myself:
True spiritual beauty;
A heart of giving;
Grey eyes with pools of true meaning.

Janet Donaldson, from *Pocket Celtic Prayers*

Once you have made up one or two triads, you will probably remember them for years. Threes really are very easy to remember.

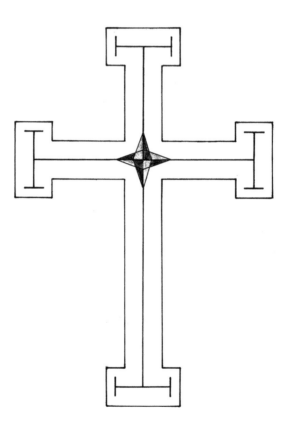

going on pilgrimage today

BLESSED ARE THOSE WHO HAVE SET THEIR HEARTS ON PILGRIMAGE. PSALM 84:5

introduction

The great danger now is that Celtic sites are overrun with those who are tourists rather than pilgrims, with all the crass commercialism that brings. It is always quite difficult to know what to expect before arrival. At most sites the atmosphere will be quite different in winter or summer, and when it is crowded or deserted. We need to remember how ascetic the Celtic missionaries were: to visit on a cold, grey, lonely February day may be more helpful than during the summer holidays!

The second thing to remember is that any remains seen today may well not be from the Christian Celtic era. At Whitby, the remaining monastic ruins are from centuries later. At Whithorn, the remains tend to be archaeological and in a museum. On Iona, one sees an abbey rebuilt this century. At Escomb, the Celtic church stands, but surrounded by a twentieth-century estate. At Burgh Castle, nothing remains of Fursey's monastery, but the huge walls of the Roman fort from which he took his building material are still there. At Bradwell, Cedd's chapel remains but no other monastic buildings can be seen, and what was once forested area is now very open. On Lindisfarne the priory remains are from a later era and the most evocative place can be on the little adjacent St Cuthbert's island.

On the other hand, it is good to remember that Cuthbert fled to his island to escape the crowds, and that what now can appear to be peaceful, isolated havens were once bustling monasteries. So a sense of realism is called for – not an escape into a romantic fantasy.

In each case, it is to be remembered that a true pilgrimage is about what goes on within the inner self. Go to see, to imagine, to learn, to meditate, to pray and to try to identify the principles behind these special places that can be translated for today. Above all, go ready to be changed by the God who lives in these places, and who also lives with you where you spend the rest of the year.

What follows is just a very small selection of some of the sites worthy of a visit. There are hundreds of others. The hope is that some indication might be given of how religious tourism and gentle pilgrimage differ. Those going on pilgrimage or organizing group visits are encouraged to read these pages in conjunction with the section above on *The pilgrimage of life* (p. 114).

íona

From **Oban** the ferry takes you to **Mull**, which you cross by coach on a poor road, and then there is a further small ferry from Mull to Iona. As you draw near to the island the image of the present rebuilt abbey will become clearer. The disembarkation point is near **Martyrs' Bay** where tradition has it the Vikings slaughtered a large number of the Celtic monks. Spend time there to consider the cost of early coastal monasticism and reflect on what we owe these men of faith.

You will then be reminded of the contribution of the female saints as you walk past the ruins of the thirteenth-century **nunnery** (no doubt reflecting on the fact that in his own day Columba allowed no women on Iona). **Maclean's Cross**, which you will pass, is only about four hundred years old, but a fine example of carving. **St Oran's chapel** near the abbey takes its name from a cousin of Columba who was buried alive (willingly) in order to consecrate the ground, but, you will be glad to know, was dug up again and found to be still alive!

You will then take the **'Kings' Walk'** across the churchyard, reflecting on the tradition of how many Scottish and Scandinavian kings are buried here. One of the most moving graves at which to pause for thought is that of the great Labour Party leader, John Smith. **St Martin's Cross** (seventeen feet high) and **St John's Cross** will impress by their sheer scale, knotwork patterns and biblical scenes. The torr, a large mound just to the east of the abbey is reputed to be the site of **Columba's cell.**

The **abbey** itself, rebuilt by George Macleod and helpers this century, was founded about AD 1200 and has an atmosphere all its own with good information, an excellent bookshop and fine examples of stonework in the museum. The small shrine to the north of the main entrance is identified as the place Columba was laid to rest, and this is quite possible. Each day of the week different themes are taken for the simple but moving times of worship, led by different members of the community, and the emphasis on justice, peace and international affairs effectively prevents the visitor being lulled into a romantic escapism.

Those who stay on the island can join a **pilgrimage** each Wednesday with a member of the Community which will take in the site of a hermit's cell, a disused marble quarry, St Columba's Bay (traditionally the place Columba landed on arrival from Ireland), and other places. The pilgrimage will take most of the day and at each stop there will be prayer, information and singing. It is an experience not to be missed.

To stay on the island is most certainly to be preferred to a hurried day trip, where little of the atmosphere can be taken in, and to stay with the Community taking part in a rhythm of work, worship and rest is an experience few will forget.

Lindisfarne

The Celtic monastery was founded here by Aidan in AD 635, although there is archaeological evidence of much earlier settlements. Today little remains of Aidan or Cuthbert's time, but there are splendid fragments of stone knotwork carving in the modern **museum** which is well worth a visit. The **castle**, which dominates the landscape, dates from the sixteenth century; the ruins of the **priory** (with its distinctive skeleton of an arch) date from about AD 1150; and the **parish church** was built about AD 1250. Within the church is a small exhibition of the Celtic Christian legacy, and the woven **carpet** in the sanctuary (based on a design taken from St Mark's Gospel in *The Lindisfarne Gospels*) is not to be missed! Near both the abbey and the church is a very striking **sculpture of St Aidan** holding a blazing torch and a pastoral staff. Photographers have a field day here! It becomes quickly obvious, however, that historic Celtic scenes are unlikely. But that is not the point.

To reach Holy Island one needs to be aware of the tides, for it is cut off from the mainland twice a day. To allow the place to speak involves going with the ebb and tide of the sea, the seasons, the cycle of nature. It is only then that the rhythmic life of prayer and mission from the place begins to make sense and to offer insights into our own lives. To stay on the island, and so be able to experience it after all the tourists have disappeared, will make all the difference. A day-visitor can only ever really be a tourist rather than a pilgrim.

The nearby **St Cuthbert's Island** with its small recess in the ground invites the imagination to enter into the life of a hermit's cell – it is quite special. Here the tidal movements seem even more visible and important, the remoteness and isolation become apparent, and the presence of God is easy to grasp. Get there before anyone else!

On the mainland can be seen **Bamburgh Castle**: this is not the castle Aidan saw, but it makes obvious the link between religious and political power – separate yet keeping an eye on each other, and each mutually available. Inland from Lindisfarne is **St Cuthbert's Cave** from which both Holy Island and Bamburgh castle can be seen, and it may well have been from here that the Celtic saint mused on the relationship between the two – as does the modern pilgrim today.

A little further south at **Seahouses** boat trips carry passengers to the **Inner Farnes**, from where Cuthbert had to be lured to become a bishop against his better judgement. Ferry-men today talk more about Grace Darling and the birds than our Celtic heritage. But at the right times of the year you may see thousands of puffins and at nesting time you may have to tread with care, their numbers are so vast. Imagination and meditation, together with a knowledge of the stories of the saints, will make all the difference.

JARROW, monkwearmouth and hexham

Roughly on a line along Hadrian's Wall, these places will draw a curious variety of responses from those who visit them.

St Peter's, **Monkwearmouth** and **St Paul's**, **Jarrow** were originally sister houses at a time when Celtic monasteries were overflowing: in AD 716 these twin houses had over 600 monks.

Founded in AD 674 by Benedict Biscop, the church at **Monkwearmouth** hosts, behind its original tower and doorway, an excellent simple exhibition about a number of Northumbrian saints. It was here that Bede first entered the monastic life at the age of seven. But he remained for only two years before the new monastery at Jarrow was built, and he was taken there by its founder, Ceolfrith.

Nearby at **Jarrow**, built in AD 681, the church of St Paul still boasts some remaining walls from later monastic life. Its claim to fame, however, is that it was here that Bede wrote his *Ecclesiastical History*. Here one can see a striking modern wooden statue of Bede, and 'Bede's Chair', but this is dated at not more than 1100 years old. Good exhibitions are available and school parties are well catered for with hands-on experience of costume and monastic life.

With an injection of European funds, **Bede's World** has recently expanded, and now offers not only an historical exhibition, but is also developing a more contemporary approach demonstrating how life might have been for Bede and his society.

Further inland is **Hexham Abbey**. This foundation is the work of Wilfred (AD 634–709) much of whose original abbey lies buried today, although the seventh-century crypt is open. It was, of course, Wilfred who engineered so much of the background to the Synod of Whitby in AD 664, having been trained on Lindisfarne but who was then so attracted by the church life he saw on the continent. At Hexham is **Wilfred's Chair**, and seated in that the visitor may be inclined to try to enter the mind of Wilfred whose life and ambitions were so turbulent.

In visiting these places, we are confronted with Bede the scholar, the austere monks, the flamboyant Wilfred, and a modern attempt to reconstruct history. One begins to wonder how we ever unravel the twisted threads of historical and spiritual development.

whithorn

Whithorn is a small and delightful fishing harbour out of everyone's way in Galloway, south-west Scotland. It is hard to imagine now that here in AD 397 St Ninian built his **Candida Casa** (the White House) which was to be the first Celtic monastic community from which all others would trace their roots.

Today, as you pass through a sixteenth-century archway in the main village street, there is a superb **Heritage Centre**. This offers both a 'slide and sound' presentation which is excellent, and informative guided tours of the site. Here visitors are shown where early wooden huts were sited, where remnants of a thick whitewashed wall were found, and there is a superb display of early Celtic carved crosses: they are quite breathtaking. Most of the **priory church** ruins date from the sixteenth century and are associated with the powerful mediaeval monastery which sold its questionable theology in the form of dubious relics and papal bulls, simply trading on the heritage of Ninian.

Further along the coast is the thirteenth-century **St Ninian's Chapel** marking the place where pilgrims first landed en route to his site. There is also **St Ninian's Cave** which can only be reached by footpath, and time must be allowed for this. In this cave lots of crosses carved on stones were found, and these have now been transferred to the heritage centre. Crosses marked on the walls of the cave have nearly all now been obliterated by more modern graffiti-artists, unfortunately. On the beach all around, the smooth grey pebbles contain thin seams of white quartz. Often stones with seams intersecting each other forming a cross can be found, and these make good visual aids for reflecting on Ninian's message – and our own.

It seems that Ninian set about his work of sharing the light of Christ from this 'shining white house' in the heartland of the Druidic culture. There is little evidence of violence between the two and Ninian appears to have been peacefully successful in his mission in Scotland, his successors even engaging as far as the Orkney and Shetland islands in the sixth century.

Here is a place to be inspired by knowledgeable staff at the heritage centre and then to reflect quietly at the cave.

whitby, hackness and coldingham

It was at **Whitby** that the formidable Hilda was overseer of the mixed community of men and women, and here that she hosted the important Synod of Whitby in AD 664. Today, the **abbey ruins** stand like a stark skeleton on the high hill overlooking the modern seaside resort. Here it was that Hilda encouraged the unschooled cowherd Caedmon to develop his gift of poetry and song, and now the huge **Caedmon's Cross** stands as a monument to this man and his patron.

Archaeologists have found evidence of Hilda's community founded in AD 657, and there is a good **Heritage Centre**. But the ruins which are so dominant today are from the thirteenth century. Indeed, the original Celtic monastery ended abruptly in AD 867 when the Danes invaded and sacked so many of the coastal settlements. It is, however, still possible to allow the imagination to recreate the simple early days on that windswept headland, and marvel at the spiritual discipline encouraged there, and compare our own often rather more comfortable (and less effective?) approach.

As the attacks continued so some monks sought refuge at **Hackness,** chosen in AD 680 by Hilda as an outpost for her community. Today, this peaceful and secluded village provides the environment for a good display of Celtic stonework kept in the **parish church**. Little is known about the place except that it was from here a nun called Begu saw a vision of light and angels carrying the soul of Hilda to heaven the very night she died in Whitby. The challenge of this holy place is to meditate on how far we are able to allow God to invade our imaginations with dreams at night and visions by day – for often what he wishes to communicate is surely beyond words.

Further north beyond Lindisfarne is another place famous, or rather infamous, for its Celtic women! At **Coldingham** is the site where Ebba founded her convent and monastery about AD 655 . However, its claim to fame lies in the damning report recorded by Bede that the residents were totally unconcerned about the state of their souls, and were more taken with sleep, gossip, eating and drinking. The nuns in particular were reprimanded for weaving fine clothes and dressing to attract the attention of passing men! Cuthbert did a lot of teaching here, and it was at Coldingham that Cuthbert went out one night to stand in the North Sea, praying with his hands outstretched. Was this an early form of a cold shower after staying at this debauched place? Nothing of that era remains today, but to visit and consider the perils as well as the blessings of the Christian life can be salutary as one overlooks the dramatic scenery of the North Sea coastland.

escomB ano OuRham

A journey to these two places, only a few miles apart, will elicit an extraordinary diversity of reactions.

At **Escomb**, just south of Durham, the pilgrim will find an intact church from the period of the Celtic saints about whose early history nothing is known! Surrounded now by a twentieth-century housing estate it stands as a tiny monument to the spiritual determination of its builders. Much of it is built from remains of Roman buildings (including high on one exterior wall a sixth-century Roman Legion stone), and it is set in a traditionally Irish circular churchyard. The architecture is typical of the period: tall and narrow, indeed narrowing as the walls ascend. Two original round-headed and two original square-headed windows can still be seen, as can a Saxon sun-dial. Anglo-Saxon glass has been found on the site, and various pieces of sculptured stone are on display. Other incised crosses and patterns can easily be seen.

The church has recently produced a delightful little collection of illuminated texts entitled *The Book of Escomb*. The key to the church is available from a nearby house. It is a wonderful oasis to visit, and set as it is surrounded by ordinary modern life, the pilgrim cannot help but reflect on the fact that our Celtic heritage is for application in our contemporary society: it is not an escape from it!

By complete contrast the visitor can visit **Durham Cathedral** on the same day. It is ironic that Cuthbert, who *so* wanted not to be venerated, and *so* wanted just a simple chapel, should finally be laid to rest here with one of England's grandest cathedrals built over his remains. At one end of the building is the **tomb of Cuthbert**, where one cannot help but wonder if he would rather have finally been laid to rest in somewhere less grand like Escomb?

At the opposite end of the cathedral the **tomb of Bede** can be seen: to stand here is to be overwhelmed with gratitude for all this man recorded about the Celtic churches – he is our primary source for stories about so many of the saints.

The **ecclesiastical museum** at Durham should not be missed. On display is the **coffin of Cuthbert** which seems tiny, while the jewelled ornaments found inside his coffin seem most elaborate. There is also a fine display of Celtic crosses, including wonderful copies of the magnificent Bewcastle and Ruthwell Crosses. These are housed in the **Monks' Dormitory**.

Visit both Escomb and Durham. They each owe their spiritual significance to the Celtic Christian era. One has maintained its original simplicity while the other has been magnificently overlaid by subsequent generations. The pilgrim will judge each according to personal taste, character and need.

Bradwell and Lastingham

To reach the chapel built by Cedd at **Bradwell** in AD 653 today, one needs to travel by car to the edge of the Dengie peninsula in Essex, continue beyond the modern village, and park at the end of the road. From there it is a ten minute walk to the **chapel** which stands like an isolated barn. Inside the simple benches face the modern stone altar-table in which are set three large stones: one from Iona, where Aidan was taught; one from Lindisfarne where Aidan taught Cedd: and the third from Lastingham where Cedd built another monastery.

Here there were once a huge crumbling Roman fort, many huts belonging to the monastery, and thick trees. All of this has now gone except the chapel. The land is flat and deserted, with the exception of the **nuclear power station** a couple of miles away. It is interesting to muse which of the two, the nuclear station or the chapel, is the *real* power station, and which will last the longest! The visitor can turn 360° with almost nothing interrupting where the sky touches the ground, the land touches the sea, time touches eternity, and heaven touches earth.

To the south amongst one clump of bushes there is a tiny remnant of the old Roman walls, while beyond the field to the north are the modern buildings of the **Othona Community**. A small core community lives there while a further 400 live dispersed around the country. Theme weeks and weekends are run throughout the year and the door of hospitality is always open.

Once a year, in July, thousands converge for the annual ecumenical pilgrimage, and wonder how this deserted building has survived the ravages of North Sea weather, flood, use by smugglers, a time as a lighthouse and then a barn, and now this century rededicated as a place of worship. The clue lies in Bede's account of how Cedd went on to build his other monastery at Lastingham in the North Yorkshire moors.

At **Lastingham**, not many miles inland from Whitby, Cedd prayed and fasted for 40 days before building one stone upon another. The very ground was claimed for God, despite it being thought only fit for 'wild animals and robbers'. It is sobering to ask whether our modern church sites will be on ground so soaked in prayer that they still help people in their spiritual journey thirteen centuries from now!

Lastingham is a secluded village for the contemporary visitor in which the church is built on the site of Cedd's monastery. In the centre of the church are stairs to the crypt where beside the altar is the site where Cedd was laid to rest after he died of the plague, having acted as interpreter at the Synod of Whitby in AD 664. It was his brother Chad who assumed leadership of the community after him.

Both places are not easy to find, but will reward the visitor with a sense of peace, security and the presence of God.

on pilgrimage
in ireland

Christianity found its way to England during the later centuries of Roman rule. This had little influence on Ireland, where the only links with the Roman Empire were by trade, and, as the empire collapsed, by piracy and slave-trading. It was not until the time of Patrick, in the fifth century, that the island saw widespread and rapid Christian conversion.

Initially it was attempted to establish bishoprics on the continental pattern, which followed that of Roman civic rule, but this failed. The attraction of the monastic ideal led to the growth of monasteries, some of which used ancient sites, as it seems happened at **Kildare** in central Ireland where Brigid established her monastery. Others appear to have grown up around the dwelling of a hermit, deep in the forests. The name *diseart* (desert) still marks some of these sites, though the forests which provided the isolation have long since gone. Island or coastal sites were also occupied. The larger monasteries provided not only for celibates but for married men and their families, and they also attracted craftsmen and employed farm workers. These centres would have provided for the pastoral needs of the surrounding countryside. Women's foundations were far fewer, and, with some notable exceptions, tended to be short-lived, probably because women could not own land. When visiting these sites it is important to use the imagination and wander back in time.

In Ireland this pattern of monastic life survived until the twelfth century, when most adopted the various continental rules, though a few continued until the Reformation.

One such survivor, it is thought, was **Glendalough** in the Dublin mountains, which is easy to reach and may provide a starting point for the modern traveller. The ruins of the early Irish and mediaeval buildings attract many visitors but remain a place of peace. The site at the Upper Lake is usually less crowded than the main buildings and a number of walks lead up into the mountains.

An astonishing ancient site which can give pause for reflection is at **Grangefertagh**, near the main Dublin to Cork road. It is not easily missed, for the countryside is flat and the round tower is the highest in Ireland. While there are no other remains of the ancient monastery, there are the ruins of the mediaeval church, in which, later on, the Protestant gentry were buried. Outside lie the more recent graves of Catholics, and beside them is a working farm. Most amazingly, in the middle of this century, the church transepts were strengthened with concrete and made into a handball court. The combination of the ancient and the modern, the sacred and the secular, may make this a useful stopping place.

In the far south-west, eight miles from the coast of Kerry, is Sceilg Mhicil, or **Skellig Michael**, a great pyramid of rock rising straight from the sea-bed for some 1100 feet. On a ledge near the top are the ruins of an early monastery, comprising beehive huts, a small cemetery, and a mediaeval church. The rock can only be reached by small boat in good weather and there are no facilities for staying on the island. The monastery is reached by stone steps originally created by the monks. This remote place has always been a place of pilgrimage, and the difficulties of the journey combined with its spectacular position, can make a visit to this site an event not lightly undertaken. It is not suitable for those who experience sea-sickness or vertigo.

There are a number of other remote sites on the west coast and islands. The most famous pilgrimage occurs on the last Sunday of July each year, when thousands of people travel to **Westport** in County Mayo, and then to nearby **Croagh Patrick**. While the festival has pre-Christian origins as a celebration of the beginning of harvest, legend has it that on this mountain St Patrick fasted and prayed. It is not uncommon to climb the mountain barefoot, but, while not high, the ascent can be difficult, and the upper reaches are of slippery shale. Nineteenth-century pilgrims carried stones up the mountain with them, from which the chapel on the summit was built. In recent years, 'famine roads', roads walked by people in search of food during the Irish Famine of 1845–7, or built by them in return for their food, have been re-opened near the foot of the mountain. Some people start the pilgrimage by first walking these roads, in memory of those who starved, and in prayer and penitence for those dying of famine in the world today.

Also associated for centuries with both St Patrick and penitential practice is **Lough Derg**. Pilgrims arrive at the lake having fasted since midnight, and are taken by boat to Station Island. Everyone then takes off their shoes and embarks upon a round of set prayers in the open, around 'beds', the remains of beehive huts. The first night is taken up by a vigil in the church; on the second night it is permitted to snatch some sleep if possible. Food is minimal, consisting of bread and black tea. Pilgrims leave on the third day, replacing their shoes but remaining fasting until midnight. While the modern routine is strongly Roman Catholic in tradition, pilgrims of all backgrounds report that the experience of being the same as each other, in the open, cold wet and hungry, can give a powerful sense of being in communion with the poor and downtrodden of the world.

Further west in County Donegal is **Glencolmcille**. Many ancient remains scattered around the valley are associated with St Columba, and there is an annual pilgrimage. On a much smaller scale, holy wells can be found throughout Ireland, some well-known, some hidden, some the scene of an annual 'pattern' (patronal day), and some all but forgotten. The modern pilgrim may wish to pause in these places, frequented down the centuries mainly by the poor and anonymous. It may be the time for the pilgrim to linger where prayer has been – and remains – valid.

© Rosemary Power

on pilgrimage in wales

Many sites of the ancient Celtic Christian communities are to be found around the south coast of Wales. The first, both in time and in significance, was that at **Llanilltyd Fawr** (Lllanwit Major). To the west of Cardiff, this was Wales' earliest centre of learning. There David, Samson, Gildas and Patrick received their training. Today the parish church which stands on the site shows little of those days. Passing through Swansea, turn south onto the picturesque Gower Peninsula. Three places of interest here, which are linked to each other, are **Oxwich** where there is a church dedicated to Illtyd, and **Llangennith** where Cenydd, a disabled pupil of Illtyd, founded a community, and **Llanmadoc** where Madoc settled and was greatly helped by Cenydd.

As you travel further west, Tenby provides the stepping off point for a visit to **Caldey Island**. Because of the huge number of visitors it is wise to cross early in the day (the time is determined by the tide). David, Illtyd and Samson all stayed for a time on the island. Today, the Cistercian monastery dominates the small island settlement and their daily offices can be experienced from the gallery of the chapel. By being present at more than one of these, a real feeling for the daily prayer-rhythm, an important feature of Celtic Christian spirituality, can be experienced. It is also possible to be taken on a guided tour of the monastery, but this is only open to men and boys!

Further along the Pembrokeshire coast, the site of an Irish Celtic hermit can be visited. Take a detour from Pembroke out towards the army ranges of Castle Martin. (Check that the road is open because on firing days there is no access). Drive out to **St Govan's Head**. From the car park look for a path down the side of the cliff to St Govan's chapel. This simple stone structure houses the original oratory of Govan, who came to live here late in life. Below the chapel is his well whose waters were famed for curing failing eyesight.

In West Wales **St David's** cathedral with its mediaeval ruins is situated on the site that David chose for his monastic community, a recognised pagan sacred site. On some Sundays in the summer a local historical society enact the history of place from the point of view of mediaeval pilgrims. The pilgrimage walk using *A Pilgrim's Manual* by Brendan O'Malley will take you on a thirteen mile walk around the headland, stopping at places of special significance, such as **St Non's chapel** (where David was born) and **Capel y Pistell** (where he was baptised). You may also enjoy a boat trip out to **Ramsey Island**, on which the companion of David, Justinian (Stinian) lived an austere life. The island is now a bird reserve and access is restricted.

Ten miles from Fishguard is the small village of **Nevern**. The church there is dedicated to St Brynach. In the churchyard there is a spectacular high cross with a Celtic design on it, as well as some other carved stonework dated from the fifth century.

Inland ten miles, on the A484, is the village of **Cenarth** which straddles the River Teifi. Here is situated the **National Coracle Centre** with a fascinating collection of coracles from around the world. This form of transport was central to the journeying exploits of the Celtic saints and the centre is well worth a visit. A route north through the middle of Wales will take you to another place with associations with David. The small town of **Llandewi Brefi**, north of Lampeter and off the A485, has a church on a raised piece of ground echoing the story of his preaching there that was so powerful that the earth rose! In the church are some interesting Celtic stones which have an Irish connection.

In the north one of the most delightful places is the small chapel at **Pennant Melangell** situated two miles up a narrow lane from Llangynog on the B4391 south of Bala. Here an Irish hermit, Melangell, came to find her 'desert place' in the seventh century. She was discovered by the local prince whilst out hunting, as the hare being chased found refuge beneath her skirt. The dogs, recognising her special quality, refused to come near. This impressed the prince so much he gave her land and a small community was founded and this place continues to exercise a ministry of care today.

On the Llyn Peninsula are places like **Llangybi** with its well, **Llangwnnadl** dedicated to St Gwynhoedl and **Aberdaron** where the church remembers St Hywyn, cousin of St Cadfan, who founded the monastic community on Bardsey Island. The latter two are part of a chain of pilgrim churches that runs down the north coast of the peninsula from Bangor to Bardsey Island. Also en route is the site of a major Celtic monastic community founded by St Beuno at **Clynnog Fawr.** The huge church, in which is situated a chapel on the site of the original, is well worth a visit and whilst of later construction somehow echoes the towering quality of the learning that epitomised St Beuno's ministry.

For those with sea-legs a visit to **Bardsey Island** will be a real experience. It is possible to stay on the island which is called the Island of 20,000 Saints, as so many came to live and die there.

At the other end of the pilgrim route is **Bangor** which gets its name from the wattle fence that St Deiniol placed round his cell in the sixth century when he came from Scotland. He became one of the major Welsh saints, refounding the community at Bangor Iscoed which had once been a major Druidic centre. A drive across the bridge onto the **Isle of Anglesey** enables you to meet two Celtic saint 'chums', St Seriol at **Penmon** north of Beaumaris where his cell and well are found in a small peaceful walled garden, and St Cybi whose base was at the other end of the island at **Holyhead**. They apparently frequently met in the middle of **Llanercymedd** to drink the holy water and to talk. Back on the mainland, a trip to **St Asaph** takes you to another cradle of Celtic Christianity, founded by St Kentigern, the founder of Glasgow. It is a fitting reminder that the spiritual history of these sister-lands is as intertwined as the Celtic knotwork patterns themselves.

© Adrian Leighton

on pilgrimage
in cornwall

Many Cornish places derive their names from the Celtic saints who brought Christianity to them. The seaside resort of **St Austell** remembers the Breton saint who founded a community there. **St Mawes** remembers another saint whose well, famed for its healing powers, can still be seen in the town. **St Ives** is associated with St Ia, an Irish nun who sailed to Cornwall. In all these places the church will usually be the focus today, but many of them were rebuilt in the nineteenth century. However, it is not the building that provides the link with the special Celtic spirituality but the place. To appreciate what that means requires time for us to spend not just looking at the features of the church but *being* at a holy place, where God can be met in a special way. Ideally the more popular places need to be visited before or after the touring coaches disgorge their occupants.

In the fifth and sixth centuries, a number of Welsh Celtic missionaries came to the north coast of Cornwall. Many of these were children of the Welsh Christian King Brycham (who gave his name to the town of **Brecon**). Many of the villages with saints names in this area are connected with this family and are found scattered either side of the A39 between Camelford and Wadebridge. Examples are **Advent** Church (St Adwen), **St Teeth**, and **Davidstow** (St David) which also has a holy well. At **St Mabyn** note the pub sign in the village of the same name! The area around Tintagel and Boscastle also reflects the strong tie with Christian Wales. Here you will come across saints like St Petroc, a relic of whom is jealously guarded in **Bodmin** Church. Not to be missed also is **St Piran's Chapel** – a simple structure set in a wood. And nearby is **St Nectan's Glen** at the top of which is St Nectan's Kieve (or hermitage).

Moving inland the isolation of **Bodmin Moor** was an attractive 'desert place' for the more solitary minded. Of particular note is St Clether's Chapel, a short walk from the parish church and village of **St Clether**. The chapel which is of a simple design has the unusual feature of a water channel running behind the altar from one side of the church to the other. Outside, there is a well with a spring where the water enters and another well where it leaves the church. The whole of the moor is covered with standing stones and the later Christian presence is marked by the pilgrim wayside Celtic crosses which are in the typical Cornish 'wheel-head' shape.

Further down the coast, the busy fishing port of **Padstow** marks the place where St Petroc established an important Christian community. Further along the coast near **Perranporth** is St Piran's Oratory. Use a map to reach it, for it is now marked by a granite plinth as it lies under the drifting sand covered in concrete! The little church at **Perranzabuloe** contains a model of St Piran's Oratory.

The south-western area of the county saw concerted evangelism by Irish monks, a large party of whom arrived under the leadership of one Fingar. Fearing attack by Irish pirates, the

Cornish king Teudal killed many of them, including Fingar on the beach in the **Hayle Estuary**. However, a number did survive and village names across the peninsula give evidence to their lives such as **Breage** (St Beacca) as do the early stone crosses in the church-yards here and at **Phillack**. Other places worth visiting are **Germor** (St Germoe), **Wendron** (St Wendrona), **Sithney** (St Sithni), **Crowen** (St Crewenna), **Gwithian** (St Gothian), **Gwinear** (St Gwinear), **Phillack** (St Piala), **St Erth**, **Levant** (St Euny) and, of course, **St Ives** (St Ia).

Further into the peninsula we can trace back our spiritual blood-lines to pre-Christian times if we are prepared to walk. A good route begins at **Sancreed** with its ancient church and stone crosses, going on to **Carn Euny**, with its ruins of an iron age village complete with 'fogue' or underground passage. Nearby is the holy well and small **chapel of St Euny**. Here in May people come to the well seeking healing, leaving pieces of coloured material or 'clouties' as a token of their prayer. Another place where you will also find these ancient prac-tices is at the well and chapel of St Madron, a mile or so outside **Madron** near Penzance. As you walk you pass a high granite wheel-head cross called the **Brane Cross**. Further remains of our ancient past lie near **St Buryan**, named after another fifth-century Irish saint. A visit to **St Michael's Mount**, a definite site of early Christian significance, is well worth the experience, even if only for walking off a few pounds up the steep path!

Along the south coast we come across both native Cornish and Breton saints. You should not miss the beautiful church at **St Just-in-Roseland**. Here Justin, son of the Cornish king Gerraint, founded his hermitage situated by the River Fal. This place still exudes the typical Celtic Christian qualities of simplicity, oneness with its surroundings, and harmony with the tides and times. At **St Winnow**, founded by a Welsh missionary, the church nestles by the estuary of the River Fowey. This river marks one end of the 'Saints Way', an ancient trading route across the peninsula which saved travellers braving the treacherous seas around Land's End and the Lizard. It serves as a good reminder that these early Christian heroes brought the Christian faith here at considerable risk to their lives. The modern pilgrim has it very easy by comparison!

© Adrian Leighton

Recommended Reading

General

Bede, *Ecclesiastical History of the English People*, Penguin, 1990.

Ian Bradley, *The Celtic Way*, Darton, Longman & Todd, 1993.

Courtney Davies, *The Book of Celtic Saints*, Blandford, 1995.

Esther de Waal, *A World Made Whole*, Fount, 1991.

Esther de Waal, *The Celtic Way of Prayer*, Hodder & Stoughton, 1996.

John Finney, *Recovering the Past*, Darton, Longman & Todd, 1996.

Richard Fletcher, *Who's Who in Roman Britain and Anglo-Saxon England*, Shepherd-Walwyn, 1990.

Michael Mitton, *Restoring the Woven Cord*, Darton, Longman & Todd, 1995.

Edward Sellner, *Wisdom of the Celtic Saints*, Ave Maria, 1993.

Philip Sheldrake, *Living between Worlds*, Darton, Longman & Todd, 1995.

Ray Simpson, *Exploring Celtic Spirituality*, Hodder & Stoughton, 1995.

Whitley Stokes, translator, *Lives of Saints from Book of Lismore*, Llanerch, 1995.

Thomas Taylor, *The Celtic Christianity of Cornwall*, Llanerch, 1995.

Shirley Toulson, *The Celtic Year*, Element, 1993.

Robert Van de Weyer, *Celtic Fire*, Darton, Longman & Todd, 1990.

Robert Van de Weyer, *Celtic Gifts*, Canterbury Press, 1997.

Worship resources

David Adam, *BorderLands*, SPCK, 1991.

Alexander Carmichael, *Carmina Gadelica*, Floris, 1992.

Iona Community, *Wee Worship Book*, Wild Goose, 1989.

Iona Community, *Worship Book*, Wild Goose, 1991.

Iona Community, *The Pattern of Our Days*, Wild Goose, 1996.

Iona Community, Song books: *Enemy of Apathy*, Wild Goose, 1988; *Heaven Shall Not Wait*, Wild Goose, 1987; *Love From Below*, Wild Goose, 1989.

Ray Simpson, *Celtic Daily Light*, Hodder & Stoughton, 1997.

Ray Simpson, *Celtic Worship Through The Year*, Hodder & Stoughton, 1997.

Martin Wallace, *Pocket Celtic Prayers*, Church House Publishing, 1996.

Art and craft

Arthur Baker, *Celtic Hand – Stroke by Stroke*, Dover, 1983.

Courtney Davies, *The Celtic Art Source Book*, Blandford, 1988.

Courtney Davies, *Celtic Borders and Designs*, Blandford, 1992.

Courtney Davies, *Celtic Stained Glass Colouring Book*, Dover, 1993.

Gaynor Goffe, *Calligraphy Step-by-Step*, HarperCollins, 1994.

Muncie Hendler, *Celtic Punch-out Gift Boxes*, Dover, 1994.

Paul E Kennedy, *Fun With Celtic Stencils*, Dover, 1995.

Aidan Meehan, *Celtic Design series (A Beginner's Manual; Knotwork; Animal Patterns; Illuminated Letters;* and *Spiral Patterns)*, Thames & Hudson, 1991-3.

John G Merne, *A Handbook of Celtic Ornament*, Mercier, 1989.

Mallory Pearce, *Celtic Borders on Layout Grids*, Dover, 1990.

Mallory Pearce, *Decorative Celtic Alphabets*, Dover, 1992.

Mallory Pearce, *Celtic Stickers and Seals*, Dover, 1995.

Mallory Pearce, *Celtic Tattoos*, Dover, 1995.

Andy Sloss, *How to Draw Celtic Key Patterns*, Blandford, 1997.

Andy Sloss, *How to Draw Celtic Knotwork*, Blandford, 1995.

Co Spinhoven, *Celtic Charted Designs*, Dover, 1988.

Co Spinhoven, *Twelve Celtic Bookmarks*, Dover, 1995.

Alice Starmore, *Celtic Needlepoint*, Collins & Brown, 1996.

Angela Wainright, *Celtic Cross Stitch Samplers*, Cassell, 1996.

Stewart J Wilson, *Celtic Gift Labels*, Dover, 1993.

Pilgrimage

Tom Davies, *The Celtic Heart*, Triangle, 1977.

Elaine Gill and David Everett, *Celtic Pilgrimages: Sites, Seasons and Saints*, Blandford, 1997.

Mick Sharp, *Holy Places of Celtic Britain*, Blandford, 1997.

Shirley Toulson, *Celtic Journeys*, Fount, 1995.

useful music resources
tapes and cds

Most of these contain a selection of gentle music which could be played before, during or after a time of worship; or as background during a workshop.

Duck Baker & friends, *The Music of O'Carolan*, Shanachie Records.

Patrick Ball, *Celtic Harp*, Vols 1, 2 & 3, Fortuna Records.

Derek Bell, *Carolan's Favourites*, Claddagh Records.

Alec Finn, *Blue Shamrock*, CBM Ltd; Atlanta Records.

Sammy Horner, *Celtic Praise*, Vols 1, 2 & 3, Kingsway (earthy songs, not gentle music).

Ann Heyman and Alison Kinnaird, *Irish and Scottish Harp Music*, Temple Records.

Ron Korb, *Tapestries*, Oasis Productions.

Annie Mawson, *Angel Voices Ever Singing*; *If You Stand Very Still*; *Where Primroses Grow*, The Old Post Office, Tirril, CA10 2JE.

Michael & Eilish, *Visions of Ireland*, Sun Street Studio, Tuam, Galway.

Hilary Rushmer, *Skylark*, Vols 1, 2 & 3; *Celtic Voyage*; *Celtic Mist*, 5 Orchard Rd, Lymm, WA13 9HH.

Sileas, *Harpbreakers*, Lapwing Records.

Various Artists, *Celtic Legacy*, *Celtic Odyssey*, Narada Productions.

Celtic Expressions of Worship: 1. *Be Thou My Vision*, 2. *The King of Love*, Kingsway.

191

índex

pocket
celtic
prayers

Martin Wallace

This handy-sized book is ideal as a resource for worship leaders, or for use in small groups. The attractive binding and cover design makes it a lovely gift! Available from all good Christian bookshops, or direct from the publishers on tel: 0171 340 0276.

0 7151 4878 8   £4.95